Telling God's Story
Year One Activity Book:
Meeting Jesus

Student Guide and Activity Pages

© 2010 Olive Branch Books

ISBN 978-1-933339-47-4

This book is to be used in conjunction with *Telling God's Story, Year One Instructor Text and Teaching Guide*; ISBN 978-1-933339-48-1

Photocopying and Distribution Policy

Art Credits:
Page 115: Used by permission of Hope Gallery, Salt Lake City, UT www.hopegallery.com
Page 219: Philadelphia Museum of Art/Art Resource, NY
Page 233: Uffizi Gallery, Florence/Art Resource, NY
Page 269: Used by permission of the National Gallery of Art, Washington, DC
Page 357: Scala/Art Resource, NY
Page 403: Used by permission of the Art Institute of Chicago

Table of Contents

Using This Student Guide

This Student Guide is designed to accompany *Telling God's Story: Year One Instructor Text and Teaching Guide*, by Peter Enns (ISBN 978-1-933339-48-1). It expands on the lessons in that book, providing coloring pages, projects, games, and memory work. Some of these activities provide opportunities to put the lessons into practice; others help the student experience the customs, geography, clothing, or culture of the New Testament world; still others reveal the ways in which artists in different eras have depicted biblical stories. For each lesson in the *Instructor Text*, this *Student Guide* contains at least two activities (sometimes three or four), and a coloring page. In addition, a series of Memory Work activities runs throughout the entire year; by the end of the school year the student will have memorized the names of Jesus' twelve disciples and the books of the New Testament.

The directions for each activity contain a list of the necessary materials, but you will also find a comprehensive list of materials on page xi.

A Typical Week in This Curriculum

Aim to complete one lesson per week. Each lesson in the *Instructor Text* opens with a brief word of explanation to the parent; this will help you in helping your children process the content of the lessons. You should spend a few moments reading the parent section ("What the Parent Should Know") from the *Instructor Text* the night before the lesson so you can ponder a bit; or if you prefer, read it right before the lesson so it is fresh in your mind—whatever works for you. The important thing is that you spend some time becoming familiar with the information so you can be of more help to your children. The purpose of these parent sections is to orient you to the biblical passage for that day. The parent sections are more detailed and complex than the scripted lessons; this will give you a broader handle on the issues surrounding the passage. It will also give you a greater vantage point from which to look at the lesson itself and, perhaps, to address questions that might come up.

Next, you may wish to read the scripted lesson from the *Instructor Text* to the student on the first day as he or she colors the coloring page for that lesson in the *Activity Book*, and then to complete projects on the second and third days. Alternately, you may read the scripted lesson on the first day, complete the coloring page on the second, and complete a chosen project on the third.

In a group setting that meets once a week, plan to read the scripted lesson as the students color and then to conclude the day's study with one of the projects or games especially suited for group or classroom use (see the list of these projects on pages xv–xvi).

Photocopying and Distribution Policy

Additional copies of the student pages (coloring pages, mazes, craft templates, etc) are available as PDF downloads. To purchase them, visit our website, www.olivebranchbooks.net, click on

"Buy the Books," and look for "Year One Activity Guide Student Pages."

For families: you may make as many photocopies of the student pages as you need for use WITHIN YOUR OWN FAMILY ONLY. Photocopying the pages so that the book can then be resold is a violation of copyright.

Schools, co-ops, and churches MAY NOT PHOTOCOPY any portion of this Activity Guide. Smaller schools sometimes find that purchasing a set of the pre-copied student pages for each student is the best option. Or you may purchase a license ($100 per volume, per year) that allows unlimited school, church, and co-op duplication. For more information, please contact Peace Hill Press: email info@peacehillpress.com; phone 1.877.322.3445.

Materials List

This materials list includes craft and unusual items that may need to be acquired ahead of time. It does not include ingredients for recipes, items which are very likely to be found around the house (such as stuffed animals, old T-shirts, toothpicks, etc.) or the following common school supplies which are used multiple times and should be on hand: construction paper, school glue, tape, scissors, crayons, colored pencils.

Item	Lessons Needed
8½" x 11" notebook	11
Aluminum can	19
Aluminum foil pan	33
Baby powder	22
Balloons at least 9" around	3
Bible	25, 29, 31, 35
Brown paper lunch bag	8, 13
Cinnamon stick	36 (optional)
Circular saw or jigsaw	30 (for optional Toolbox project)
Colored sidewalk chalk	16(optional), 25 (optional)
Colored sand	10
Compass (drafting)	3
Craft glue	14
Craft sticks	28
Dice	23
Disposable cups	5, 10, Supplemental Lesson 2
Disposable plates	3, 5, 10, 11, 20, 29
Double-sided tape	Supplemental Lesson 1
Embroidery needle	1 (optional)
Embroidery thread	1 (optional)
Empty soap box	7
Fabric glue	1, 25
Fabric square	25
Felt, 8½" x 11"	1
Flashlight	36
Flower petals	36
Foam Sheet, 5½" x 8"	25
Food coloring	7, 10, 13 (optional), 16 (optional)
Glad Ware Mini Round container with lid (4 oz. size) OR baby food jar with lid	36

Globe with lines of latitude 12, 27
Glue stick ..... 1, 4, 6, 10, 11, 15, 22, 28, 29, 30 (optional), Supplemental Lesson 2
Gold Glitter ..... 7 (optional), 20, 22, 27 (optional), 31
Gold/silver crayon ..... 1 (optional)
Hammer ..... 12, 30 (for optional Toolbox project)
Hole punch ..... 7, 11, 23 (optional)
Legos 30
Lemon juice 32
Magnet 25
Marshmallows & mini-marshmallows 5, 35
Masking tape 1, 5
Matzo bread 36
Mineral oil 7
Mustard seeds 3
Nails (1") ..... 30 (for optional Toolbox project)
Newspaper ..... 5, 10 (optional), 13 (optional)
Origami paper 31
Paint, brown 14
Paint, powder tempera 25
Paint, silver, suitable for plastic ..... 10 (optional)
Paintbrush 1, 10, 11, 14, 16, 25, 31, 32
Photo album, small 15
Pipe cleaners, green 33
Plaster of Paris mix 33
Plastic Easter eggs, 6 4
Plastic sea creatures ..... 7 (optional)
Plastic bottle, ½-liter, empty 3
Plastic soda bottle, 1 or 2-liter, empty 7
Play-dough ..... 5, 7 (optional), 22
Playing cards, 1 or 2 decks 17
Plywood or scrap wood, ½" thick ..... 30 (for optional Toolbox project)
Poster board, green, 2-3 sheets 32
Potting soil ..... 3, Supplemental Lesson 2
Recording of "O Come, O Come Emmanuel" 21
Recording of *Sanctus* 33
Recording of "We Three Kings of Orient Are" 22
Ribbon, 8" 25
Ribbon, thin, 10"-12" 3
Ribbon, wide purple ..... Supplemental Lesson 1
Rubber/latex gloves 13
Rubbing alcohol ..... 10 (optional), 36
Sandpaper ..... 30 (for optional Toolbox project)
Sandwich baggie, resealable 12, 29
Saw ..... 30 (for optional Toolbox project)
Sharpie marker ..... Supplemental Lesson 3
Shoebox 4, 28, 30
Stones ..... Supplemental Lesson 3
Straight edge ..... 30 (for optional Toolbox project)

Group/Classroom Activities

These activities are particularly suited to group or classroom settings, though many of the others would be appropriate as well. In addition, every lesson in this book contains a coloring page for students to color.

Lesson 1: Make Roman Coins, Find the Lost Coin
Lesson 2: Unscramble the Judges, Praying Hands Mobile
Lesson 3: What Is Yeast?, Make a Mustard Seed Tree, Plant Mustard Seeds
Lesson 4: What Is a Tax Collector?, Make a "What God Does for Me" Collage
Lesson 5: Find the Lost Sheep
Lesson 6: Water and Wine Jars, Memory Work
Lesson 7: Make a Boat
Lesson 8: Make a Basket of Loaves and Fish
Lesson 9: "Walking on Water" Maze, Why Does it Sink or Float?, Memory Work
Lesson 10: Make a Centurion's Helmet, Centurion, May I? game
Lesson 11: Watercolor Blessing, *Christ and the Children* Notebook, Give a Blessing
Lesson 12: Light and Dark game, Polar Night
Lesson 13: Build a Bird's Nest, Memory Work
Lesson 14: Make an Ox Yoke, Make the Ten Commandments Tablets
Lesson 15: Make Jesus' Family Tree
Lesson 16: Grow Salt Crystals, Salt and Soda Overflow
Lesson 17: Oath Red Light/Green Light, "Cheat" Game, Memory Work
Lesson 18: Respond Jesus' Way, Showing Kindness
Lesson 19: First-century Clothing Paper Dolls
Lesson 20: "Seek and Find" Word Search, Memory Work
Lesson 21: Birth of Jesus Scavenger Hunt, Picture Study of Tanner's *The Annunciation*, "O Come, O Come, Emmanuel"
Lesson 22: The Gifts of the Wise Men, "Follow the Star!" game, Make a Star
Lesson 23: Fleeing into Egypt game, Escape to Egypt Comic Strip
Lesson 24: Crack the Code, Make Coins from the Time of Herod the Great, "Return to Israel" Maze
Lesson 25: Go Fishing game, Duccio's *The Calling of the Apostles Peter and Andrew*, Fishers of Men game
Lesson 26: Don't Judge on Appearances game, Praying for Others, Memory Work
Lesson 27: Where Are You From?, Make a King's Crown
Lesson 28: "Serving God" Match-up, Show Hospitality
Lesson 29: Map of the Temptations of Jesus, Label Herod's Temple
Lesson 30: Build a Synagogue, Learn Something New about a Person You Know, Memory Work

Materials for Group/Classroom Activities

This materials list includes craft and unusual items that may need to be acquired ahead of time. It does not include ingredients for recipes, items which the students' parents are likely to have on hand (such as stuffed animals, old T-shirts, toothpicks, a Bible, etc.) or the following common school supplies which are used multiple times and should be on hand: construction paper, tape, scissors, a stapler, pencils, crayons, colored pencils, glue sticks, and school glue. You will also need copies of the workbook pages for each student. For copying and licensing information, see the copyright page of this book.

Item:	Lessons Needed
5-oz. tub of play-dough, any color (or make salt dough from the recipe in the Lesson 7 activities)	22
9 inch rubber balloon	3
A few baby food jars with lids OR GladWare Mini Round container with lids (4 oz.size)	36
Aluminum foil	7, 22, 25
Any of the following: self-adhesive gems, beads, buttons, pasta shapes, glitter or glitter glue	27
Appetizing snack for the students, set in a plain, old, beat-up box	26
Assorted leaves (if you have time, give the students a bag and let them go outside and gather them)	15
Audio recording of "O Come, O Come Emmanuel"	21
Audio recording of "We Three Kings of Orient Are"	22
Audio recording of choral version of the *Sanctus*	33
Baby doll	22
Baby powder	22
Baking chocolate	26
Baking pan	16
Big bowl (e.g., punch bowl, your largest mixing bowl)	25
Brightly colored scraps of paper (stamps, gift wrap, scraps of wrapping paper or construction paper, magazine clippings, or photographs)	11 (optional)
Brown paper lunch bag	8
Buckets	13
Cardboard (some thin, such as a cereal box, and some thick/corrugated)	1, 10, 14, 16
Cardboard or cardstock, 9" x 12"	Supplemental Lesson 2
Clear jar (without lid)	16
Compass (drafting)	3
Craft glue	14
Crown (toy crown, or make your own using the template from Lesson 27)	22

Unit 1
Stories Jesus Told

Lesson 1: God Is Joyful over You

Activities

Game Activity: **The Lost Coins and the Secret Message**
History Project: **Make Roman Coins**
Craft Project: **Make a Coin Pouch**
Game Activity: **Find the Lost Coin**
Coloring Page: **A Woman Searches for Her Lost Coin**

Game Activity
• •
The Lost Coins and the Secret Message

Materials

- Large rimmed cookie sheet (or a large box lid)
- 10 quarters
- Masking tape
- Fine-tipped marker
- Sand or cornmeal (enough to fill the cookie sheet)
- Paintbrush (½"- to 1"-wide brush works best)
- The Lost Coins and the Secret Message (Student Page 7)

Directions

1 Tear out Student Page 7. Arrange the 10 quarters randomly on the cookie sheet. Stretch a small piece of masking tape across the top of each quarter to secure it.
2 Write a number and a letter on the tape that is covering each quarter, as follows: 1 H, 2 E, 3 I, 4 S, 5 J, 6 O, 7 Y, 8 F, 9 U, 10 L.
3 Fill the cookie sheet with the sand or cornmeal. Each quarter should be completely covered.
4 Have the student use the paintbrush to sweep away the sand to find the ten coins. After she finds each one, have her fill in the numbered blank on Student Page 7 with the letter on the coin. The message revealed answers the question: *How does God feel when a person comes to know Him?* (Answer: HE IS JOYFUL.)

2

History Project

• •

Make Roman Coins

The ten silver coins the woman owned were probably Greek drachmas or the Roman equivalent, denarii (say deh NAR ee). Each one of these was about a day's wage for a laborer. In this project the student will make her own Roman denarii, and in the next project she will make a pouch to keep them in.

Materials

- Scissors
- Gold or silver crayon or colored pencil
- Glue stick
- Sheet of cardboard (the back of a legal pad, or the front and back of a cereal box, for example)
- Model of Roman denarius coins (Student Page 9)

Directions

1   Color the ancient Roman coins on Student Page 9 a gold or silver shade, and cut them out. (If you want to use these same designs for the backs of the coins, photocopy the page first, and then cut out all ten. Actual denarius coins often had different designs on each side, but we've chosen simplicity over exactness here.)
2   Using the blank circle as a template, cut out five disks from the cardboard.
3   Use the glue stick to glue each paper "coin" to a cardboard disk. This will make it more durable than paper alone.
4   Now that you have five coins, you can use them with the next activity.

Note to Instructor: If the student is curious about any of these, the five designs are (top row, left to right) Mark Antony, veiled because he is mourning for the dead Julius Caesar; Mark Antony, unshaven because he is in mourning; Livia, mother of the emperor Tiberius, holding an olive branch and flanked by Tiberius's title of PONTIF[ex] MAXIM[us]; (bottom row, left to right) the Temple of Jupiter, which Augustus Caesar built in Rome; a winged representation of Victory holding a clipeus virtutis or "shield of bravery" (an award for soldiers who had shown bravery in battle) and flanked by the initials SPQR (for Senatus Populusque Romanus, "The Senate and the People of Rome").

Craft Project

. . . .

Make a Coin Pouch

Materials

- 8" x 11" piece of felt, any color
- Pouch pattern (Student Pages 11 and 13)
- Dark marker
- Fabric glue or hot glue gun
- Velcro Sticky-Back Coin (⅝")
- OPTIONAL: Embroidery thread and needle

Directions

1 Cut out pouch pattern on Student Pages 11 and 13.
2 Trace the pattern onto the felt. Cut out felt pieces.
3 Using the fabric glue or hot glue gun, apply a line of glue to three sides of the bottom felt piece (see the markings on the illustration at right).
4 Attach the other felt piece. Press to seal.
5 Attach the Velcro Sticky-Back Coin to the felt pieces to create a closure. For a more secure closure, glue the coin to the felt (instead of relying on the stickiness). Wait for the glue to dry. Now you have a secure place to keep your coins.
6 OPTIONAL: When the glue is dry, you can embellish your pouch by using a needle and thread to create decorative stitching around the outside edges.

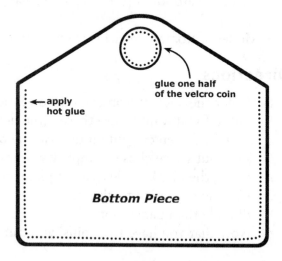

glue one half of the velcro coin

←apply hot glue

Bottom Piece

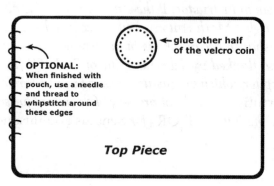

←glue other half of the velcro coin

OPTIONAL: When finished with pouch, use a needle and thread to whipstitch around these edges

Top Piece

Game Activity

. . . .

Find the Lost Coin

Materials

- 1 quarter (or you may use a denarius from the previous activity)

Directions

1   Have one person cover their eyes while another hides a coin out of sight.
2   Once the coin is hidden, the person uncovers her eyes and looks for the coin while the others give hints like "cold," "warm," "hot," etc. Since coins are so small and difficult to find, you may need to provide more hints as the person gets close (such as, "look high," "look under," "look between," etc.).
3   When the seeker finds the coin, she gets to be the one to hide it for the next person.
4   Repeat the activity until everyone has had a chance to hide the coin and look for it.

Coloring Page

. . . .

A Woman Searches for Her Lost Coin

Jesus' parable tells of a poor woman who loses a coin in her small house, and lights a lamp to search intently until she finds it.

The Lost Coins
and the Secret Message

How does God feel when a person
comes to know Him?

_____ _____ _____ _____
  1   2   3   4

_____ _____ _____ _____ _____ _____.
  5   6   7   8   9   10

Make Roman Coins

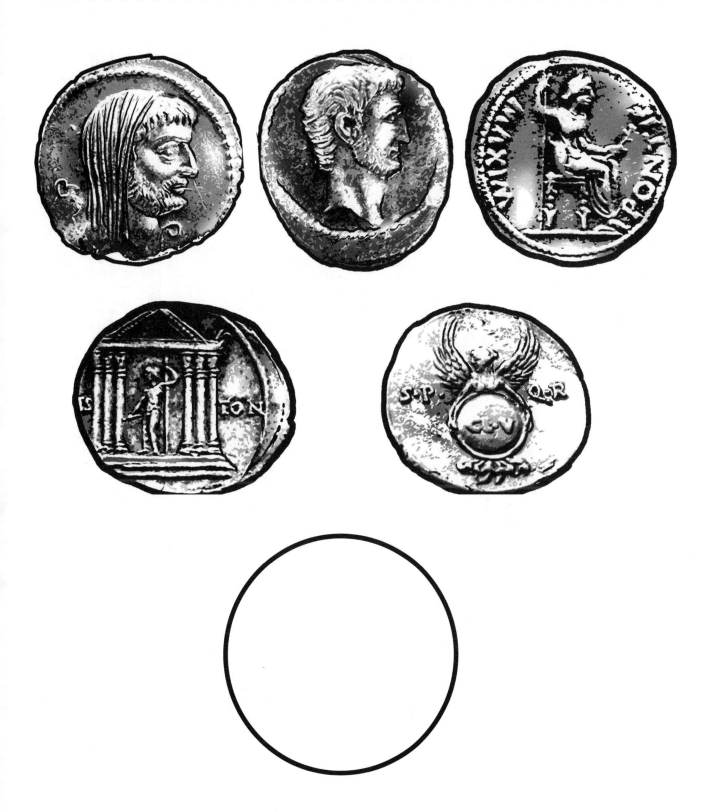

Pouch Pattern Part 1

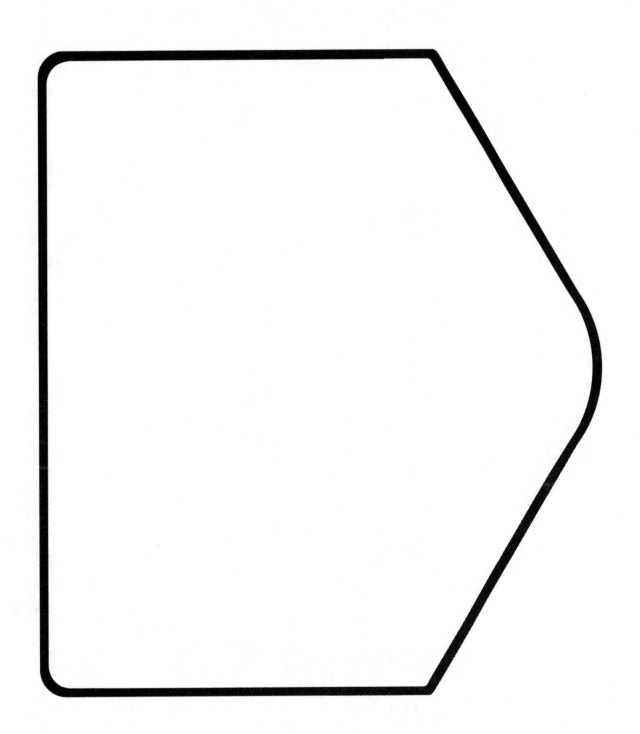

Pouch Pattern Part 2

Luke 15:8–10

Lesson 2: Don't Give Up When You Pray

Activities

Game Activity: **Unscramble the Judges**
Craft Project: **Stained-glass Praying Hands**
Craft Project: **Praying Hands Mobile**
Coloring Page: **A Widow Begs a Judge to Help Her**

Game Activity

· ·

Unscramble the Judges

Materials

- Judges' qualities cards (Student Page 21)
- Scissors
- Pencil
- Paper

Directions

1 Turn to Student Page 21. Read through the left-hand column, telling the student for each phrase, "This is what God is like." Then read through the right-hand column, telling the student for each phrase, "This is what a bad judge is like."
2 With the student's help, cut out all the cards and mix them up.
3 Have the student divide the cards into two piles: those statements that describe the bad judge from the parable and those that describe God, the ultimate judge. See if he can remember, based on your read-through from the beginning of the activity.
4 Once the cards are sorted, the student should write the circled letters from each pile onto his paper. The letters from the bad judge cards will form the first word, and the letters from the God cards will form the second word, giving the completion of this sentence: In Jesus' time, the judges in Jerusalem were so bad that people gave them the nickname of *Dayyaney Gezeloth*, which means _____ - _____. *Answer: Robber-Judges*

17

Craft Project
. . . .
Stained-glass Praying Hands

Materials

- Wax paper
- Crayon shavings (shave bits off crayons with a crayon sharpener, scissors, or knife)
- Pencil
- Scissors
- Paper (colored or plain)
- Markers
- Clear tape
- Iron
- Paper towel

Directions

1   Tear off a sheet of wax paper. Fold it in half. This folded piece should be larger than the student's hand.
2   The student should trace his hand in pencil onto the wax paper. The fingers should be slightly spread apart.
3   Open the wax paper so it is unfolded. Arrange the crayon shavings on one side of the paper. You can also write "Always pray and don't give up" in marker on a slip of paper and place it over the shavings. Fold the top half of the wax paper down again.
4   Heat the iron on low. Place a paper towel over the wax paper and iron until the crayon shavings melt. Let cool.
5   Cut out the hand from the wax paper. You now have a stained-glass effect. Tape the praying hands to a window to let the light shine through.

Craft Project
. . . .
Praying Hands Mobile

Materials (for each student)

- Wire coat hanger
- String or yarn
- Glue
- 3 pieces of colored construction paper
- Scissors
- Marker

Directions

1 Cut each piece of construction paper in half crosswise and lengthwise to make four equal rectangles.

2 With the marker, have the student trace his hand, fingers together, onto the construction paper. (If you have the time, you can have the student cut out the tracing. Keep in mind he will be doing this 12 times.)

3 The student should make a hand tracing for each of the remaining paper rectangles. He should alternate tracing his left and right hand.

4 Cut six pieces of string, three short (about 8") and three long (about 16").

5 Pick a "pair" of hands that, when placed back to back, look like praying hands. Apply some glue to the back of one hand and place the end of the string on the glue. Put the back of the other hand overtop to sandwich it in place. Repeat for the remaining pairs of hands.

6 Tie the ends of the string pieces to the clothes hanger to create your mobile. Pray with the student today, and tell him to hang his mobile in his room to remind him to talk to God.

Coloring Page

· ·

A Widow Begs a Judge to Help Her

Jesus told a story of an unkind judge who would not help a poor widow. Jesus said that God isn't like that judge; God will answer us when we pray.

Unscramble the Judges

People pray to him day and night.

Ⓙ

He may or may not listen to someone who comes to him.

Ⓑ

He is fair.

Ⓤ

He takes a long time to give justice.

Ⓑ

He listens right away.

Ⓔ

He doesn't respect God.

Ⓞ

He always listens to those who come to him.

Ⓓ

He is bothered by those who come to him.

Ⓡ

He gives justice quickly.

Ⓢ

He only gives justice to keep from being bothered.

Ⓡ

He wants people to come to him.

Ⓖ

He doesn't respect men.

Ⓔ

Bad Judge Letters

___ ___ ___ ___ ___ ___

God Letters

___ ___ ___ ___ ___ ___

In Jesus' time, the judges in Jerusalem were so bad that people

gave them the nickname of *Dayyaney Gezeloth*, which means

_____ - _____.

Luke 18:1-8

Lesson 3: Small Beginnings, Big Results

Activities

Cooking Project: **Mustard Seed Mashed Potatoes and Quick Yeast Bread**
Science Activity: **What Is Yeast?**
Craft Project: **Make a Mustard Seed Tree**
Science Activity: **Plant Mustard Seeds**
Coloring Page: **The Great Tree**

Cooking Project
. . . .

Mustard Seed Mashed Potatoes and Quick Yeast Bread

These recipes allow the student to see and handle mustard seeds (they are incredibly small) and observe the effect of yeast on dough. Let the student help you in the kitchen—children love mashing the potatoes and kneading the dough. Add a saucy roast from the crock pot and you have a great dinner.

MUSTARD SEED MASHED POTATOES

Ingredients

- 5 lbs. Yukon Gold potatoes
- 1 Tbsp. + 1 tsp. salt
- 4 Tbsp. butter
- ½ c. chicken broth or vegetable broth
- 1 c. sour cream
- ¼ c. Dijon mustard
- 2 Tbsp. mustard seeds (Can be purchased at www.thespicehouse.com; most grocery stores carry them too. Note that you cannot use this type of mustard seed for the "Plant Mustard Seeds" project.)

Directions

1 Peel the potatoes if desired. Then have the student help you cut the potatoes into chunks and place them in a large pot. Add cold water to cover by at least one inch. Add 1 Tbsp. of salt (reserve the other teaspoon).
2 Bring to a boil. Boil 20–25 minutes until tender.
3 While the potatoes are boiling, melt the butter in a small saucepan over low heat. Let the student help you add the chicken broth and stir.
4 Drain the potatoes in a colander and return to the pot. With the student's help, add the butter-broth mixture, sour cream, Dijon mustard, and mustard seeds to the potatoes. Then together, mash the potatoes until they are the consistency you like.

QUICK YEAST BREAD

Note: You can make this bread in your mixer with a dough hook, but we recommend doing it the old-fashioned way so the student can have fun "working the yeast in the dough," just like the woman in the parable.

Ingredients

- 5–6 c. white flour (bread flour works best)
- 2 Tbsp. white sugar
- 2 pkg. (2 Tbsp.) quick-rising active dry yeast
- 1 tsp. salt
- 1 c. warm water (about 120 degrees F.)
- Oil or cooking spray
- OPTIONAL: 2 Tbsp. olive oil or melted butter

Directions

1 Mix together sugar, yeast, salt, and 4 cups of the flour in a large bowl.
2 Add the warm water. Have the student help you mix the water in.
3 Gradually add 1 cup of the remaining flour until the dough is no longer sticky. You may need to add more flour if it is a humid day.
4 Flour or oil your hands. Place the dough on a floured surface and knead for 5 minutes. The dough should be stretchy and smooth—not sticky.
5 Put the dough back in the bowl and cover with a damp dish towel. Let it rise for 30 minutes. While the dough is rising, preheat an oven to 400 degrees. When the dough has risen, punch it down.
6 Let the student help you grease two loaf pans. Divide the dough in half and place each half in a loaf pan. Let rise until the dough is level with the rim of the pan.
7 Bake for 40 minutes. Remove bread from pan and let cool on wire rack. If desired, brush the top of each loaf with olive oil or melted butter.

Science Activity

What Is Yeast?

Materials

- 1 empty half-liter water bottle
- 1 c. warm water
- 1 pkg. rapid-rise active dry yeast
- 3 tsp. sugar
- 9-inch rubber balloon
- Rubber band

Directions

1 Tell the student, "In this week's lesson, Jesus said that just a tiny bit of yeast can change a big lump of dough. We're going to see part of that process today. Dry yeast may look like sand, but it is actually a living organism that is waiting to 'wake up and eat.' Let's add some warm water to the yeast to wake it up from its sleepy state, called dormancy." Have the student pour the yeast package into the empty water bottle and add the warm water.

2 Place the cap on the bottle and have the student shake it gently.

3 Tell the student, "The yeast needs food—and it likes sugar." Help the student add the sugar to the bottle.

4 Tell the student, "When the yeast eats the sugar and breathes the oxygen in the water, it gets rid of carbon dioxide gas. Let's put a balloon on the bottle to see how much gas the yeast produces." Fit the balloon over the mouth of the bottle and secure it with the rubber band.

5 Tell the student, "The yeast eats the sugar and starts to reproduce itself and make even more yeast. That is how a little yeast can work through a whole batch of dough. As someone kneads the dough, the yeast spreads to every part of the dough, eating the sugar and dividing and dividing until there is lots of yeast in every part of the dough."

6 Check the bottle and balloon every 5–10 minutes for the next 45 minutes. Note the bubbles in the water (this shows the yeast is making the gas). When was the balloon the biggest? Once the yeast has eaten all the sugar, it will stop dividing and slip back into a dormant ("sleep") state. Tell the student, "The yeast makes the carbon dioxide gas. When yeast is mixed into dough, the gas bubbles get trapped in the sticky dough. That's what makes bread fluffy."

Craft Project

Make a Mustard Seed Tree

Materials (for each student)

- Tree template (Student Page 33)
- Marker
- Scissors
- 8" x 5½" piece of cardboard
- Compass (or another sharp object that can make a hole in foam)
- Thin ribbon (about 10–12 inches)
- School glue
- Mustard seeds (1–2 Tbsp.). These can be purchased at www.thespicehouse.com; most grocery stores carry them too.
- Disposable plate

Directions

1   Have the student cut out the tree template from Student Page 33. (If time is a factor, cut this out yourself and have it ready for the student.)
2   Ask the student to place the cut-out tree template on the cardboard sheet and help her trace the shape onto the sheet.
3   Have the student cut out the tree shape from the cardboard and glue the paper tree template onto the cardboard tree shape.
4   Help the student make a hole in the top of the tree and thread the ribbon through it. Tie the ribbon to make a loop.
5   Ask the student to place the paper/cardboard tree on the plate and use the glue to "color in" the branches section of the tree.
6   Shake the mustard seeds onto the tree (this is why the plate is there). The seeds will stick wherever there is glue. Let dry. Remind the student that a mustard seed starts small, but it grows into an enormous tree. This is like God's kingdom; it began with one man (Jesus), but is now growing and growing.

Science Activity

Plant Mustard Seeds

Mustard seeds will grow into a tall, scrubby bush, but people grow them in gardens and pick the edible leaves from the young plant. Mustard greens are nutritious, packed with vitamins A, C, and K. You can pick the leaves while they are small and put them in salads, or you can let them mature and cook the greens like you would spinach. You can grow the seedlings indoors in a sunny spot or, if the weather is seasonable (spring or early fall is best), you may wish to grow them outside.

Materials

- 1 packet of mustard seeds (Purchase at a nursery or at www.parkseeds.com. Do not use the kind sold as spices, because those may not sprout. The Mustard Savannah Hybrid is $1.50 per packet and produces mature plants in about 20 days.)
- Large pot or collection of small pots
- Potting soil
- Water

Directions

1 Have the student fill the pot (or pots) with soil.
2 Push a seed ½" under the soil. Move over 1" and plant another seed. Plant as many seeds as the space allows, as long as they are all at least 1" apart.
3 Let the student water the soil until it is moist but not soggy. Put in sunny spot.
4 Check back on the seeds every day. Add water to moisten the soil as needed.
5 When the seedlings emerge, pluck out the extras so you have one seedling every three inches. (You can clean and eat what you pull out.)
6 Keep watering and tending plants, with the student's help. These should grow fast. From planting to eating only takes about three weeks (if you planted the Savannah Hybrid).

Coloring Page

• •

The Great Tree

In Matthew 13, Jesus compares God's work on earth to a tiny seed that grows and grows into a strong tree. The tree is large enough for all the birds to come and nest in it. The birds you see in this picture are a few of the kinds that lived in Galilee in Jesus' time (and still live there today). The hoopoe (the bird with the wild feathers sticking up from its head) should be colored yellow or orange with black-and-white striped wings. Color the martins (the three other birds flying through the air) dark blue on top and white underneath. The Syrian woodpeckers (do you see them sitting on the tree branch?) would be black, white, and red.

Mustard Seed Tree

Matthew 13:31–33

Lesson 4: God Loves a Humble Heart

Activities

Craft Project: **The Pharisee and the Tax Collector Diorama**
Game Activity: **What Is a Tax Collector?**
Craft Project: **Make a "What God Does for Me" Collage**
Coloring Page: **The Pharisee and the Tax Collector**

Craft Project

. . . .

The Pharisee and the Tax Collector Diorama

This diorama is a model of a wooden carving found in a cathedral in Toledo, Ohio.

Materials

- Shoebox
- Thin cardboard (such as an empty cereal box)
- Scissors
- Tape
- 1–2 brown grocery bags (depending on the size of the shoebox)
- Glue stick
- Colored pencils
- Pharisee and tax collector cut-outs (Student Page 41)

Directions

1 OPTIONAL: Cut apart the brown grocery bag. Cover the outside and inside of the shoe box with the plain brown paper. Secure with tape.

2 Have the student cut out the pictures of the Pharisee and tax collector on Student Page 41. Color with colored pencils. (Note: Both figures are depicted in the traditional style of prayer at the time: their arms crossed over their chest. Point out to the student that the tax collector, just as he is described in the parable, can't bear to look up. He is also beating his breast as he prays, which is rare for a man of that time to do. It is an act of extreme anguish.)

3 The student should trace each figure on the thin cardboard. Cut out cardboard (if the cardboard is thick you may need to assist the student with this step).

4 The student should use the glue stick to glue the paper figures to the cardboard.

5 Have the student follow these instructions: Turn the shoebox lengthwise so it stands tall and narrow. Bend back the tabs on the top and bottom of each figure. Glue or tape the tabs to the inside of the shoebox so the figures are standing. (The Pharisee should stand in front of the tax collector.)

6 Ask the student, "Pretend that this is the temple. Look at the way each man is standing. Can you tell from their expressions and postures who is being more humble before God?"

Game Activity

What Is a Tax Collector?

Materials

- 6 treats (candy, stickers, or coins—all the treats should be the same)
- 6 plastic Easter eggs
- Tax Collector Facts (Student Page 43)
- Scissors

Directions

1 Cut out each of the Tax Collector Facts (Student Page 43).
2 Place one treat and one fact card in each plastic egg.
3 Have the student leave the room. Hide the six eggs.
4 Tell the student to come back in and find the eggs—but not to open them yet!
5 Open the eggs with the student and read the Tax Collector Facts. The student should put his treats in a pile.
6 Tell the student, "I am the tax collector, and you need to pay the Roman Empire. So I need 1 of your treats for the Romans." [Take the treat.]
7 Tell the student, "Wait, I changed my mind. The tax is higher now. I need another treat." [Take the treat.]
8 Tell the student, "There is also a special tax on people whose name begins with the letter [say the first letter of the student's name]. I need another treat." [Take the treat.]
9 Tell the student, "You don't have much left, do you? I also want another treat just for myself. I am not going to give it to the Romans. But if you don't give it to me, I'll tell the Roman soldiers that you refused to pay any of your taxes. Then you'll be arrested." [Take another treat.]
10 Discuss with the student, "Am I being nice to you?" Tell her that tax collectors did things like this, and were disliked because of it. (You can give the treats back if you're feeling extra nice.)

Craft Project

Make a "What God Does for Me" Collage

Materials (for each student)

- 11" x 17" piece of blank paper (or two 8½" x 11" taped together)
- Glue stick
- Scissors
- Markers
- Magazines (parenting and family magazines are best)
- OPTIONAL: Head-shot photograph of the student

Directions

1 Discuss what it means to be humble before the Lord (i.e., knowing that God listens to us and treats us kindly even though we have not done the things we should).

2 Brainstorm with the student about the good things God does for the student. Write these down where the student can see them. See the list below for ideas.

   What God Does for Me (examples)
   Takes care of me.
   Is always with me.
   Forgives me when I do wrong.
   Gives me food, a home, and a family.
   Tells me how to live the right way.
   Listens to me when I pray.
   Comforts me when I'm sad or afraid.

3 Cut out the student's head from the photo and glue it to the bottom of the paper (or find a picture of a child in the magazine and use that). Draw "thinking bubbles" coming up from the head of the student.

4 Find and clip pictures from the magazines that reinforce the things on the list you brainstormed. The pictures can be loose representations. For example, a picture of an ear could be used for "Listens to me when I pray." Alternately, the student can draw pictures directly on the paper.

5 Glue the pictures to the paper, and hang it on your refrigerator or in the student's room. Tell him, "This is the way to be humble. Always remember who God is and what he has done for you."

. . . .

The Pharisee and the Tax Collector

When the Pharisee prayed, he bragged to God about how good he was. That is not how God wants us to come to him. The tax collector came with the right attitude: he knew he had done bad things, but he believed that God would be kind to him.

Pharisee and Tax Collector Cut-outs

Tax Collector Facts

Tax collectors were Jews who collected money from their fellow Jews and gave it to the Roman Empire.

Tax collectors were not allowed to be judges or witnesses. They were often not allowed to worship God with the rest of the people.

Tax collectors would take more money from people than was fair.

Jesus spent time with tax collectors. People asked, "Why would Jesus want to be around those people?"

Tax collectors were called "traitors" and were hated by their fellow Jews.

One of Jesus' disciples, Matthew, was a tax collector.

Luke 18:9–14

Lesson 5: Lost Sheep

Activities

Cooking Project: **Cinnamon Roll Sheep**
Craft Project: **Make a Shepherd's Rod and Staff**
Craft Project: **Build a Sheepfold (with Sheep!)**
Game Activity: **Find the Lost Sheep**
Coloring Page: **The Shepherd Finds His Lost Sheep**

Cooking Project

• •

Cinnamon Roll Sheep

This easy recipe makes 4 sheep.

Ingredients

- 1 can (12 oz.) refrigerated cinnamon rolls (regular size, not grands) with icing
- Plastic knife
- 1 egg, beaten
- Pastry brush
- Miniature marshmallows or grated coconut
- 4 raisins or mini M&Ms
- Cookie sheet

Directions

1 Preheat the oven to 400 degrees F. Have the student grease the cookie sheet or line it with parchment paper. Open the cinnamon roll can and set the icing packet aside. *Note: Assist the student to make the first sheep. Once she has the hang of it, she can make the remaining three herself.*

2 Take 1 cinnamon roll and squeeze it a bit to turn it into an oval. This will be the sheep's body. Place the roll on a cookie sheet, cinnamon side up.

3 Unwind another cinnamon roll to get a long strand of dough. Cut off two small pieces (2 legs) and one piece double that size (the head). You can even cut off a tiny piece for a tail if you wish.

4   Dip the pastry brush in the beaten egg and brush on the top of each leg and the under-side of the sheep. Attach each leg to the sheep.

5   Fold the head piece in half to create a small oval. Brush the egg on the edge of the head and on the "neck" of the sheep. Attach the head to the sheep (so you have a sheep in profile). Do the same for the tail if you made one.

6   Make three more sheep with the remaining rolls.

7   The instructor should put the cookie sheet in the oven and bake the rolls for 8–10 minutes (until lightly browned).

8   Remove the sheep from the oven and let cool for a few minutes.

9   The student can spread the icing on the body of each sheep. Sprinkle with coconut flakes or add mini marshmallows.

10 Dab a bit of icing on the raisin or M&M and attach it to the head to make an eye.

Craft Project

· ·

Make a Shepherd's Rod and Staff

Materials

- 3 empty wrapping paper tubes
- Masking tape (wider is better)
- Newspaper
- Tissue paper (any color)
- Brown craft paper or paper grocery bags

Read the following to the student:

Today we're going to make a shepherd's rod and staff. A shepherd stayed with his sheep. Since sheep were constantly on the move looking for fresh pasture, the shepherd had to travel light. But there were two things he was never without—his rod and staff.

A rod was a shepherd's club. He used it primarily to defend his sheep against wolves or other predators. He could strike with it or throw it. The rod was also used to count the sheep as they entered the sheepfold each night and again as they left in the morning.

A staff was a shepherd's walking stick. It had a hook at one end which he could use to grab a wayward sheep (to pluck it out of a thorny bush, for example). The shepherd could also touch a sheep with the end of his staff to gently guide it back into the fold.

Directions for the Staff

1   Let the student help you tape two wrapping paper tubes together to create one long tube.

2   Twist the newspaper into a cylindrical shape, and bend to form a hook or C shape, about 5 or 6 inches from top to bottom, leaving a straight tail at one end to insert into the cardboard tube.

3   Insert the tail of the newspaper hook into the wrapping paper tube.

4   Using masking tape, cover the hook, attaching it firmly to the tube.

5   Have the student help you cover the staff with the brown paper and secure with tape.

Directions for the Rod

1 Ball up a piece of tissue paper and tape it to the end of a paper tube.
2 Cut a square of brown paper and place it over the tissue ball (so the ball is wrapped in brown). Secure the paper to the neck of the paper tube.
3 Cover the rest of the tube with brown paper and secure with tape.

Craft Project

. . . .

Build a Sheepfold (with Sheep!)

Materials

- Play dough (Use Play-Doh or help the student make the salt-dough recipe below.)
- Large disposable plastic dinner plate (like Solo brand)
- Sheep cut-outs (Student Page 51)
- Scissors
- Tape
- OPTIONAL: Sand, pebbles, dirt, grass clippings, tiny twigs, moss

SALT-DOUGH RECIPE

INGREDIENTS

- 1 c. salt
- 1¼ c. warm water
- 3 c. flour
- Plastic bag

Directions

1 In a large bowl, mix the salt with the warm water.
2 Gradually add the flour. Knead into a ball.
3 The dough can be stored overnight in a plastic bag in the refrigerator.

Sheepfold Directions

1 Say to the student, "A shepherd would let his sheep wander during the day, but at night he would lead them into a secure enclosure called a sheepfold. The sheepfold could be a cave, or a stone wall built by the shepherd. The sheepfold kept the sheep from wandering off at night and protected them from predator attacks."
2 Have the student roll the play dough into small balls (like stones that are about ½" in diameter). The student should stack the play-dough stones to make a wall that is "C" shaped. (A sheepfold always had an opening [the gate] for the sheep to come in at night and go out in the morning. The shepherd would pile branches at the opening to close in the sheep, or he himself would sleep in the gate to protect the sheep. Jesus says in John 10, "I am the gate for the sheep.")

3 If you have the optional materials (sand, pebbles, dirt, grass clippings, tiny twigs, moss), the student can embed them into the wall to make it look more realistic.

4 Have the student cut out the sheep on Student Page 51. Fold along the dashed lines, and crease along the dotted line, then tape the two halves together at the top to make standing sheep. Put them in the pen.

Game Activity

• •

Find the Lost Sheep

This is a game of observation and visual tracking.

Materials

- 3 identical, opaque plastic cups
- 1 mini marshmallow

Directions

1 On a clean table, arrange the three cups in a row. Place the mini marshmallow under the center cup and tell the student that the marshmallow is the "sheep."

2 Tell the student to watch the cup with the marshmallow closely. The student is the "shepherd," and she must keep an eye on her sheep.

3 Now it is time for the sheep to get lost. Start moving the cups, swapping the outside cups to the center position. Start by moving the cups slowly for 10 seconds. Stop moving the cups. The student should lift up the cup she believes has the marshmallow inside. Was she right? If so, move the cups longer or faster the next time.

Coloring Page

• •

The Shepherd Finds His Lost Sheep

Jesus told a story about how happy a shepherd was when he found the sheep who had wandered away from the flock. In the same way, God kindly brings us back when we wander away.

Sheep Cut-Outs

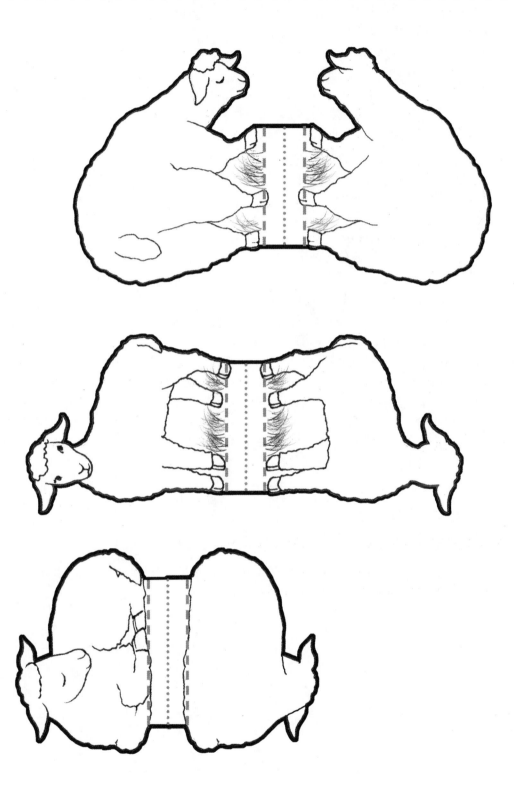

Matthew 18:12–14

Unit 2
Miracles Jesus Did

Lesson 6: Jesus' First Miracle

Activities

Craft Project: **Water and Wine Jars**
Memory Work: **The Books of the New Testament, Part I**
Coloring Page: **Jesus' First Miracle**

Craft Project

· ·

Water and Wine Jars

Materials (for each student)

- Empty toilet-paper roll
- 1 sheet brown construction paper
- Scissors
- Glue stick
- Blue tissue paper
- Purple tissue paper

Directions

1 Cut thin strips (about ½" wide and 8" tall) from the brown construction paper. (You can show the student how to do this himself, or if time is a factor, you can have these strips ready beforehand.)

2 Have the student glue one end of the paper inside the toilet-paper tube and bend the paper strip around the outside of the tube and glue the other end of the paper in the opposite end of the toilet-paper tube. The strip should appear to "bubble out" from the side of the tube.

3 Repeat step 2 with the other strips of paper until you have a rounded-looking jar.

4 Let the student crumple up some blue tissue paper and stuff it in one end of the tube (let it poke out slightly). This side represents the water.

5 Flip the tube over and have the student stuff some crumpled purple tissue paper in that end (let it overflow a bit too). This side represents wine. Now you have a craft that reminds you, when you flip it upside down, that Jesus turned water into wine!

Memory Work

- -
The Books of the New Testament, Part I

Materials

- New Testament Books, Part I: (Student Page 59)

Directions

Read the following to the student:

We read about Jesus—who he was, what he did, what he said—in a book called the Bible. The part of the Bible that was written after Jesus came is called the New Testament. The stories about Jesus that you've heard in these lessons have all come from the New Testament. The New Testament is made up of 27 smaller books, and this year, we're going to learn the names of these books.

This week we'll learn the names of five books. The first four tell the story of Jesus' life. They are named after the people who wrote them: Matthew, Mark, Luke, and John. The fifth book tells what Jesus' helpers did after he sent them out to tell everyone about him. It is called The Acts of the Apostles ("Acts" means things that people did, and "Apostles" were Jesus' special helpers), but most of the time people shorten that name to just Acts.

Listen as I say those names to you twice:

(Say two times): Matthew, Mark, Luke, John, Acts.

Now let's repeat those names three times together:

(Together, three times): Matthew, Mark, Luke, John, Acts.

Have the student tear out Student Page 59. He can decorate the sheet, and you should put it on the refrigerator or some other visible spot, to remind you and the student to review.

Coloring Page

- -
Jesus' First Miracle

When the wine at the wedding feast ran out, Jesus made more wine out of the water in the water jars. The servants were amazed!

New Testament Books, Part I

Matthew

Mark

Luke

John

Acts

John 2:1–11

John 2:14[1]

Lesson 7: Jesus Controls the Weather

Activities

Science Activity: **Sea of Galilee in a Bottle**
Map Activity: **Topographical Map of the Sea of Galilee**
Craft Project: **Make a Boat**
Memory Work: **Review the Books of the New Testament**
Coloring Page: **Jesus Calms the Storm**

Science Activity

• •

Sea of Galilee in a Bottle

Materials

- Empty plastic soda bottle (1 or 2 liter), label removed
- Oil (baby oil or mineral oil are best because they're clear)
- Water
- Blue food coloring
- Craft glue
- Funnel (you can do without this if you are careful)
- OPTIONAL: Glitter, sand, plastic sea creatures

Directions

1 The student should fill the bottle halfway with water. She should add a few drops of food coloring to turn the water blue. If you want to add glitter, sand, or sea creatures, do so now.
2 Using the funnel (this prevents mess), help the student carefully fill the rest of the bottle with oil.
3 Have the student squirt some glue around the inside of the bottle cap. Screw the cap tightly on the bottle.
4 Tilt the bottle back and forth gently to make a stormy Sea of Galilee.

Map Activity

Topographical Map of the Sea of Galilee

Materials

- Sea of Galilee map (Student Page 67)
- Scissors
- Broiler pan or rimmed baking sheet
- Aluminum foil
- Plastic knife
- Salt dough (see recipe below)

SALT-DOUGH RECIPE

Ingredients

- 1 c. salt
- 1¼ c. warm water
- 3 c. flour
- Plastic bag
- OPTIONAL: Food coloring

Directions

1 In a large bowl, have the student mix the salt with the water.
2 Gradually add the flour, enough to make a smooth (but not goopy) dough. Knead into a ball.
3 Knead in food coloring if desired, or you can paint the project at the very end. Make the dough green or brown (for brown, mix equal drops red, blue, and yellow).
4 The dough can be stored overnight in a plastic bag in the refrigerator.

Map Directions

1 Have the student cut out the Sea of Galilee from the map on Student Page 67.
2 The student should place the Sea of Galilee cut-out in the center of the pan. Now add the dough around it, shaping it into mountains that border the sea. The Sea of Galilee is surrounded by tall mountains; the highest are on the east (right) side. The actual Sea of Galilee is quite low, 680 feet below sea level. The cool dry air from the mountains mixes with the warm, moist air over the sea, and storms result.
3 Once the student is finished shaping the dough mountain range, remove the paper Sea of Galilee. Tear off a sheet of aluminum foil that is larger than the Sea of Galilee paper. Assist the student to shape the foil inside the dough basin to make an aluminum "bowl" representing the Sea of Galilee. The student should press the foil edges into the dough to seal.

4   Bake the map in a 300 degree F. oven until dry (about 1 hour). Once baked, have the student paint it if she likes.

5   The student can add a little water into the foil Sea of Galilee. The actual Sea of Galilee is quite shallow, only 200 feet at its deepest. The water is easily churned up by the wind, making storms there treacherous. Have the student blow on her sea to create waves.

Craft Project

· ·

Make a Boat

This boat really floats!

Materials (for each student)

- Empty soap box (the box a single bar of soap comes in)
- Aluminum foil
- Scissors
- Drinking straw
- White paper or notebook paper
- Crayons
- Play dough OR salt dough, small amount (to make your own salt dough, which can be substituted for play dough in several of the activities in this book, follow the recipe at the bottom of this activity)
- Hole punch

Directions

1   Have the student help you cut off one of the large sides of the soap box to make a container (imagine a shoebox without the lid).

2   Tear off a sheet of aluminum foil and place the soap box in the center. Wrap the soap box with the aluminum foil to make the boat waterproof.

3   Cut a square or a triangle (whichever shape you prefer) out of the paper. This will be the sail. Let the student decorate it if she wants to. Punch a hole in the top and the bottom of the paper.

4   Thread the drinking straw (the mast) through the holes in the paper. Take a tiny clump of play dough and stick it in the center of the boat. Stick the straw in the play dough to keep the sail upright.

5   Later the student can put her boat in the bathtub and blow it across the sea!

SALT-DOUGH RECIPE

Ingredients

- 1 c. salt
- 1¼ c. warm water
- 3 c. flour
- Blue, red, and yellow food coloring
- Plastic bag

Directions

1   In a large bowl, mix together the salt and warm water.
2   Gradually add the flour. Knead into a ball. Set aside one third of the dough.
3   Add a few drops of blue food coloring to this smaller portion. Knead the dough until it is uniform in color. Then add equal drops red, yellow, and blue to the larger portion of dough to make the color brown. Knead until brown in color.
4   The dough can be stored overnight in plastic bags in the refrigerator.

Memory Work
· ·
Review the Books of the New Testament

Directions

Say to the student: "Remember, in the last lesson we learned the names of the first five books of the New Testament. They were Matthew, Mark, Luke, John, and Acts. Let's chant those together five times."

(Together, five times): Matthew, Mark, Luke, John, Acts.

Coloring Page
· ·
Jesus Calms the Storm

The disciples were afraid of the big storm and thought their boat would sink. But Jesus made the storm stop just by telling it to stop. That showed the disciples that Jesus had God's power to command the weather.

Sea of Galilee Map

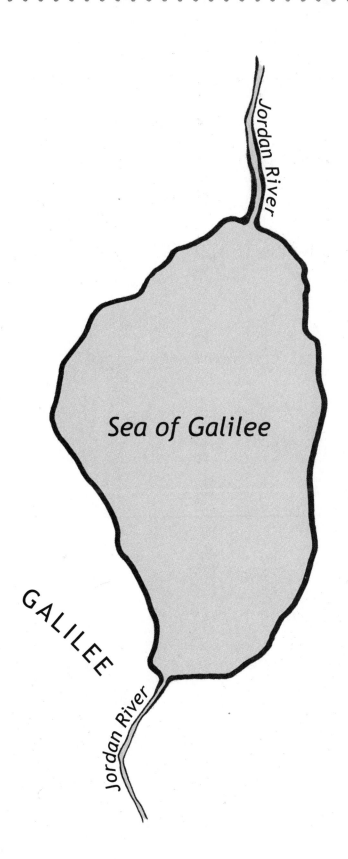

Jordan River

Sea of Galilee

GALILEE

Jordan River

Matthew 8:23-27

Lesson 8: Five Loaves and Two Fish

Activities

Craft Project: **Make a Basket of Loaves and Fish**
Cooking Project: **Loaves of Bread**
Memory Work: **Review the Books of the New Testament**
Coloring Page: **Feeding the Thousands**

Craft Project

· ·

Make a Basket of Loaves and Fish

Materials

- Loaves and Fish cut-outs (Student Pages 75 and 77)
- Crayons or markers
- Scissors
- Brown paper lunch bag

Directions

1 Have the student color the five loaves and two fish on Student Pages 75 and 77.
2 Help the student cut them out with scissors.
3 To make the basket, roll down the top of the brown paper bag (all four sides) as though you were cuffing a pant leg. Stop folding when your basket is about 4 inches deep.
4 Have the student place the loaves and fish in the basket. Now, ask the student to try to divide the loaves and fish up into as many pieces as he can. This will probably involve tearing them up into tiny bits.
5 Once they're all torn, help the student count the pieces (you'll have to take over once the numbers are higher than the student can count) and see if you have 5,000 pieces (there were over 5,000 people present at this miracle). You probably won't have nearly that many. Say, "Does each piece look big enough, by now, to make a full meal for a person? No. Jesus didn't just break up the bread into crumbs . . . he did a miracle; he made enough bread and fish for all the people to eat their fill."

Cooking Project

Loaves of Bread

This recipe is for pita bread, a flat loaf of bread made for many centuries in the Middle East (there are several types of Middle Eastern flatbread, varying from region to region, but pita is the most well known). Ordinarily, pita is baked in brick ovens, but it can be made in a home oven too.

Ingredients

- 1 Tbs. of yeast or quick-rising yeast
- ½ c. of warm water
- 3 c. all-purpose flour
- 1¼ tsp. salt
- 1 tsp. granulated sugar
- 1 c. lukewarm water
- Storage bags

Directions

1   Say to the student, "In this week's lesson, you heard that Jesus used a few small loaves to feed thousands of people. Today, you'll make some loaves like the ones Jesus may have used."

2   Dissolve the yeast in ½ cup of warm water. Have the student help you add sugar and stir until dissolved. Let sit for 10–15 minutes until water is frothy.

3   Let the student help you combine the flour and the salt in a large bowl. Make a small "dent" in the middle of the flour and pour the yeast water into that dent.

4   Slowly add 1 cup of warm water, and have the student stir with a wooden spoon or a spatula until elastic.

5   Place the dough on a floured surface and knead for 10–15 minutes, until the dough is smooth and elastic and not sticky anymore.

6   Coat a large bowl with vegetable oil and place the dough in the bowl. Turn dough upside down so all of the dough is coated. Allow to sit in a warm place for about 3 hours, or until it has doubled in size.

7   Once it is twice its original size, have the student help you roll it out in a rope, and pinch off eleven or twelve small pieces. Place them on a floured surface. Let sit covered for 10 minutes. Preheat oven to 500 degrees F. and make sure rack is at the very bottom of the oven. Be sure to also preheat your baking sheet.

8   Have the student help you roll out each ball of dough with a rolling pin into circles/disks. Each should be about 5–6 inches across and ¼ inch thick.

9   Bake each circle for 4 minutes until the bread puffs up. Turn them over and bake for 2 minutes.

10   Remove each loaf from the baking sheet with a spatula and add additional loaves for baking.

11 Take the spatula and gently push down the puff. Right away, place the bread into storage bags.

Memory Work

· ·

Review the Books of the New Testament

Directions

Say to the student: "Remember, you have learned the names of the first five books of the New Testament. They are Matthew, Mark, Luke, John, and Acts. Let's chant those together five times."

(Together, five times): Matthew, Mark, Luke, John, Acts.

Coloring Page

· ·

Feeding the Thousands

Jesus took a very small bit of food and made enough food to feed more than five thousand people! Everyone had enough to eat, and there were baskets full of bread and fish left over.

Loaves Cut-Outs

Fish Cut-Outs

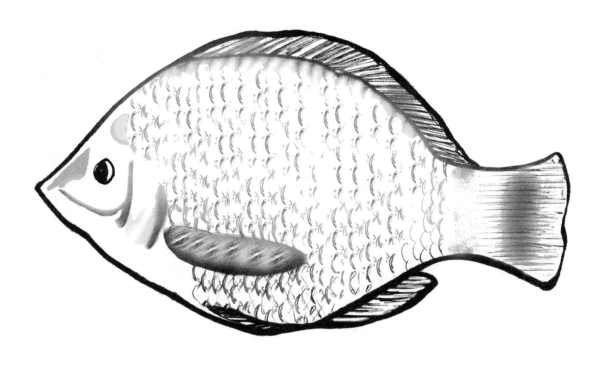

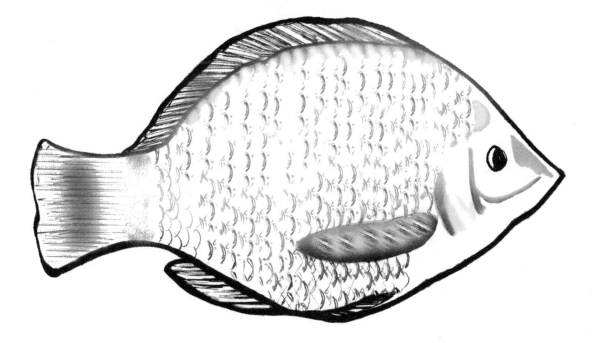

Luke 9:10–17

Lesson 9: Jesus Walks on the Water

Activities

Game Activity: **Walking on Water Maze**
Science Activity: **Why Does It Sink or Float?**
Memory Work: **The Books of the New Testament, Part II**
Coloring Page: **Jesus Walks on the Water**

Game Activity

. . . .

Walking on Water Maze

Materials

- Pencil
- Student Page 85

Directions

Have the student use her pencil to find a path from Jesus to the boat with the disciples.

Science Activity

. . . .

Why Does It Sink or Float?

When Jesus walked on water, he did something that humans cannot normally do. Do this simple experiment to see what kinds of things sink or float in water.

Materials

- Sink or Float chart (Student Page 87)
- Pencil
- Sink or bathtub full of water

Any 10 of the following

- Stick
- Rock
- Ball of play dough
- Unopened can of diet soda
- Unopened can of regular soda
- Apple
- Orange
- Grape
- Penny
- Dime
- Golf ball
- Ping-Pong ball
- Paper clip
- Plastic button
- Metal button
- Toothpick
- Cork

Directions

1 Gather the 10 items and the Sink or Float Chart on Student Page 87.
2 Ask the student to write the name of each object in the first column, if she is able (or write it for her, if her writing skills are not yet up to this task. Writing isn't the point of this project).
3 Have the student carefully place the object in the water. Does it sink or float? You or the student should record the answer in the Result column.
4 Repeat the process of testing and recording the result for the rest of the objects.
5 Discuss with the student. Which objects floated? Which sank? Were you surprised by any of the results? Why?

Note to Instructor: If the child is curious about the reasons for this, you can explain further. Objects sink or float depending on their density (mass divided by volume, or in simplified terms, how closely packed the molecules of the object are), not their size or weight. A really large log will float in water because wood is less dense than water. But a glass marble will sink because glass is denser than water.

Memory Work

· ·

The Books of the New Testament, Part II

Materials

- New Testament Books, Part II (Student Page 89)

Directions

Say to the student: "We have already learned the names of the first five books of the New Testament. Let's say those together twice."

[Together twice]: Matthew, Mark, Luke, John, Acts.

Continue reading to the student:

Today we are going to learn nine more books. These books are letters written by a man named Paul, who told many people about Jesus. He wrote letters to groups of people, and the letters are named after the people they are addressed to. So the letter to the people in the region of Galatia is called Galatians. Do you hear "Galatia" in the word Galatians? Some of the groups received two letters, so we put them together and say "First and Second _____." Here are the first five: Romans, First and Second Corinthians, Galatians, Ephesians. Let me say those again, and this time you repeat each one after me as I go. Romans *[student says "Romans"]*, First and Second Corinthians, Galatians, Ephesians. And now let's say them together three times.

[Together three times] Romans, First and Second Corinthians, Galatians, Ephesians.

Good! Now for the last four in the list of group-letters: Philippians, Colossians, First and Second Thessalonians *[say thess-ah-LOH-nee-uhns]*. I'll say those again, and you repeat each one after me as I go. Philippians *[student says "Philippians"]*, Colossians, First and Second Thessalonians. Now let's say those four, three times.

[Together three times]: Philippians, Colossians, First and Second Thessalonians.

Great job! Now we are going to put these two shorter lists together, and say all of today's list at once.

[Together three times]: Romans, First and Second Corinthians, Galatians, Ephesians, Philippians, Colossians, First and Second Thessalonians.

Have the student tear out Student Page 89. She can decorate the sheet, and you should put it on the refrigerator or some other visible spot, to remind you and the student to review.

Coloring Page
• •
Jesus Walks on Water

Jesus came to the disciples when they were afraid. He crossed the stormy lake just by walking on the water! He showed his disciples that he was more powerful than the storm.

Walking On Water Maze

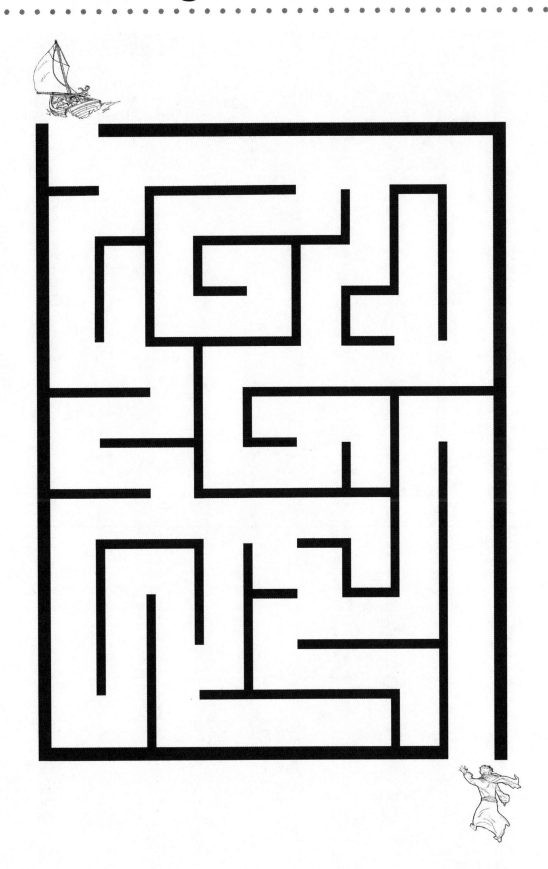

Sink or Float Chart

Object	Result

New Testament Books, Part II

Matthew

Mark

Luke

John

Acts

Romans

First and Second Corinthians

Galatians

Ephesians

Philippians

Colossians

First and Second Thessalonians

Mark 6:45–52

Lesson 10: A Soldier's Faith in Jesus

Activities

Craft Project: **Roman Centurion Sand Art**
History Project: **Make a Centurion's Helmet**
Game Activity: **Centurion, May I?**
Memory Work: **Review the Books of the New Testament**
Coloring Page: **A Roman Centurion and His Troops**

Craft Project

. . . .

Roman Centurion Sand Art

Materials

- Roman centurion head (Student Page 99)
- Colored sand or rice (at least three colors—purchase sand at a craft store, OR see recipe for colored rice below project)
- School glue (such as Elmer's)
- Water
- Spoon
- Disposable cup or bowl
- Disposable dinner plate
- Paintbrush
- Cardstock (8½" x11"—you can cut it from a cereal box)

Directions

1   Using some glue, mount the Roman centurion head (Student Page 99) on the cardstock.
2   Mix together a spoonful of glue and a spoonful of water in the cup.
3   Decide which colors you want each section of the picture to be. Paint glue on the sections you wish to be the same color.
4   Sprinkle the sand (or colored rice) on the paper and dump the excess off into the plate (then put the sand back in the container for another project).
5   Repeat steps 3 and 4 with the remaining colors of sand (or rice). You may need to mix more glue paint. Let the artwork dry.

OPTIONAL COLORED RICE RECIPE

Materials for each color

- 1 c. rice
- ½ c. rubbing alcohol
- Food coloring
- Container with lid (such as a Mason jar or an old peanut-butter jar)
- Newspaper

Directions

1 Put the alcohol into the jar and add drops of the food coloring to get the desired color.
2 Add the rice to the jar. Screw on the lid and shake!
3 Let the rice sit in the jar for 5 minutes.
4 Spread the rice on the newspaper. Move it around periodically so it all dries evenly. Pour the dried rice back in the container.

History Project

· ·

Make a Centurion's Helmet

The Roman centurion was an army officer, and his helmet had a special plume on top so he could be easily identified by his foot soldiers in battle. In this craft project, you'll make a centurion's helmet that a child can wear.

Materials

- Centurion helmet template (Student Pages 101 and 103)
- 1 gallon plastic milk jug, rinsed and dried
- Scissors
- Cardboard (we used a Capri-Sun box; a cereal box would also work)
- 2 sheets of red construction paper
- Glue stick
- Sharp knife or X-Acto knife
- OPTIONAL: Silver paint suitable for plastic*

*You have several options: (1) Use Paint for Plastic, available at craft stores, and apply with a brush. You must use the Paint for Plastic Primer as a base coat. (2) Use a spray paint such as Krylon Fusion for Plastic Metallic Shimmer, available at craft and home improvement stores. Wipe the plastic down with paint thinner first for best results. (3) You can skip the paint and cover the helmet with aluminum foil, but prepare yourself for some complicated wrapping. (4) Or you can leave the helmet unpainted. Pretend that it has been through many battles and that its original metallic sheen has faded to the color of a milk jug.

Directions

1. Cut out Plume Template A from Student Page 101. Trace the template onto the cardboard twice and cut out both pieces.
2. Cut out Plume Template B from Student Page 103. Trace the template onto each piece of construction paper and cut out both pieces. Cut the fringe into the paper plumes.
3. Fit the two cardboard plumes back to back so they match perfectly. Glue a red paper plume to the inside of each piece (so the red plume is sandwiched by the cardboard pieces and the fringe of the plume sticks up above the cardboard). Set aside.
4. Cut the opening off the milk jug with the scissors. Cut out the handle (this will be where the face opening will be). Looking at the drawing on Student Page 99, and at the diagrams below, cut the milk jug so it is shaped like a helmet.
5. Using the sharp knife or the X-Acto knife, cut a slit in the top of the helmet wide enough to stick in the stem of the cardboard plume.
6. Stick the cardboard plume into the helmet so 1 inch of the cardboard stem is on the inside of the helmet. Fold back each of the cardboard pieces inside the helmet so they lie flat against the helmet interior.
7. Paint the helmet silver or cover it with aluminum foil. The helmet will sit high up on the head, but the ear flaps will keep it in place. If you wish to widen the helmet, cut a slit up the back of the helmet to the crown.

Remove handle and spout
from milk jug by cutting
along the dotted lines
(creating two ear protectors).

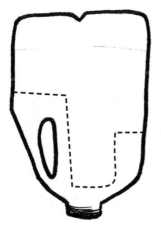

Using the X-Acto knife, cut a slit
in the top of helmet (this should run transversely across the head - from left to right
- and be just big enough for the cardboard
stem to fit in).

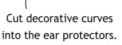

Cut decorative curves
into the ear protectors.

Insert the cardboard stems (with plumes
attached) into the slit.
On the inside of the helmet, fold back each
cardboard flap so that they lie flat and hold
the plume in place.

Game Activity
Centurion, May I?

Directions

This game is best played outside, but a large room with some open space will suffice

1 Pick one player to be the Centurion. Like the Roman centurion in today's lesson, this player gets to have "authority." He should wear the centurion's helmet from this week's projects; additionally, he can carry a small stick, as many centurions did (but unlike real centurions, the player may NOT hit other players with the stick).

2 Everyone who is not the Centurion lines up, at least 30 feet away from the Centurion. Their goal is to reach the Centurion.

3 Have the players take turns asking, "Centurion, may I _____?" (Each player chooses some request that will get him or her closer to the Centurion's location, such as "Centurion, may I take three big steps toward you?" or "Centurion, may I take 2 sideways steps toward you?"). The requests MUST always begin with "Centurion, may I" or they do not count.

4 When each player makes his request, the Centurion decides whether to say "Yes" or "No." If the answer is yes, then the player may fulfill his request. If not, he has to wait until it is his turn again. The Centurion may only refuse the request of a particular player three times per game.

5 At any TWO times in the course of the game, the Centurion may order everyone to take two steps backward. All players must obey at once. But the Centurion can only make this order twice.

6 The first player to reach the Centurion becomes the new Centurion, and the game begins again.

Memory Work
Review the Books of the New Testament

Directions

Say to the student: "Let's review all the books of the New Testament that you've learned so far. Remember, the first five books you learned were Matthew, Mark, Luke, John, and Acts. Let's chant those together three times."

(Together, three times): Matthew, Mark, Luke, John, Acts.

Say, "Then we learned about the letters that one of Jesus' messengers, named Paul, sent to different groups of Christians. There were nine of them: Romans, First and Second Corinthians, Galatians, Ephesians, Philippians, Colossians, First and Second Thessalonians. Let's chant those together three times."

(Together, three times): Romans, First and Second Corinthians, Galatians, Ephesians, Philippians, Colossians, First and Second Thessalonians.

Say, "Now let's say all of those together."

(Together): Matthew, Mark, Luke, John, Acts, Romans, First and Second Corinthians, Galatians, Ephesians, Philippians, Colossians, First and Second Thessalonians.

Coloring Page
• •
A Roman Centurion and His Troops

A centurion in the Roman army was in charge of 100 men. If he told them what to do, they did it right away. The centurion in today's story knew that Jesus was even more powerful than that. He said to Jesus, "Whatever you say will happen, happens right away." Notice how the centurion's helmet and armor look different from what the soldiers wear. He also carries a stick, to show his authority (and to hit his soldiers if they don't obey!). [The soldiers' shields can be colored red with yellow designs, and the plume on the centurion's helmet can be colored red too.]

Roman Centurion Sand Art

Plume Template A

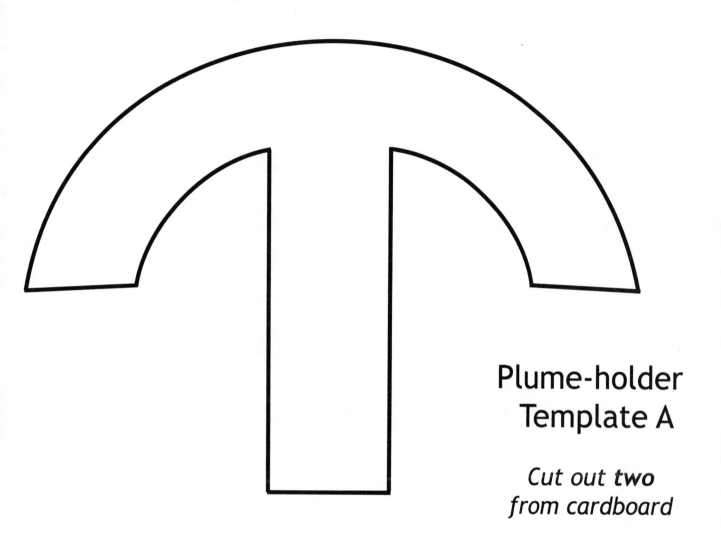

Plume-holder
Template A

*Cut out **two**
from cardboard*

Plume Template B

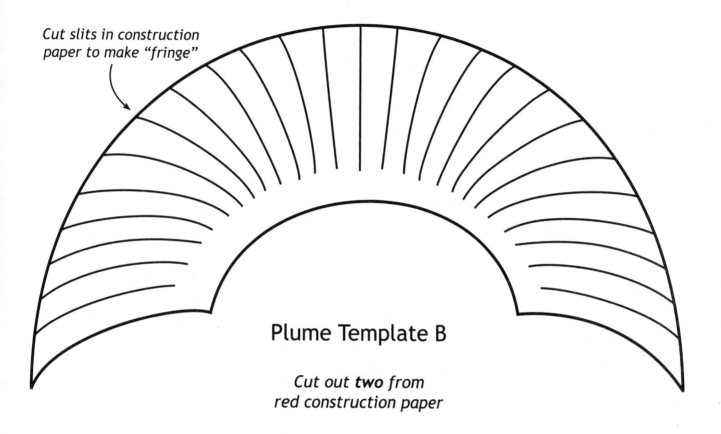

Cut slits in construction paper to make "fringe"

Plume Template B

*Cut out **two** from red construction paper*

Matthew 8:5–13

Unit 3
Teachings of Jesus

Lesson 11: Jesus Blesses and Prays for the Children

Activities

Craft Project: **Watercolor Blessing**
Craft Project: ***Christ and the Children*** Notebook
Craft Project: **"Jesus Loves Children" Heart Pocket**
Prayer Activity: **Give a Blessing**
Memory Work: **Review the Books of the New Testament**
Coloring Page: **Jesus Blesses the Little Children**

Craft Project

• •

Watercolor Blessing

There are many blessings in the Bible, but the blessing in Numbers 6:24–26 is one of the most famous.

Materials

- Blessing from Numbers 6:24–26 (Student Page 113)
- Watercolors and paintbrush set (like Crayola), and a cup of water OR crayons

Directions

1 Tear out Student Page 113.
2 Color the border with crayons or paint it with watercolors. Using the watercolors, color the blessing.
3 Put it up in the student's room or classroom.

Craft Project

· ·

Christ and the Children Notebook

This painting is by the Danish artist Carl Bloch (1834–1890). He painted 23 paintings of the life and death of Christ for the King's Praying Chamber at the Frederiksborg Castle Chapel. Although he also painted portraits and historic scenes, his paintings of Jesus are largely recognized as his artistic legacy.

Materials

- *Christ and the Children* (Student Page 115)
- Scissors
- OPTIONAL: Brightly colored scraps of paper (stamps, gift wrap, old scraps of wrapping paper or construction paper, magazine clippings, or photographs)
- Glue stick
- Crayons, colored pencils, or markers
- 8½" x 11" notebook, any color

Directions

1. Tear out Student Page 115, which contains the painting *Christ and the Children* by Carl Bloch. Show the student how Jesus refuses to send the children away, despite the disciple on the right who seems to be objecting. To see this painting in vivid color, visit the Hope Gallery website at www.hopegallery.com/php/artwork.php?artwork=688.

2. Have the student decorate our black-and-white version, on the Student Page, to look like the original. She can color the people's clothing with crayons, or she can collage the clothing using the brightly colored scraps of paper. It's all right to overlap papers, place them at an angle, or place a smaller item on top of a larger one.

3. When she is satisfied with the scene, use the glue stick, applied evenly, to glue the picture to the front of the notebook. This will make a cover that, every time she sees the notebook, will remind the child of Jesus' care for her.

Craft Project

· ·

"Jesus Loves Children" Heart Pocket

Materials

- 2 thin white paper plates
- Hole punch
- Yarn (about 2 ft.)
- Tape
- Scissors
- Markers
- Parenting magazines (they have many pictures of kids)
- OPTIONAL: Picture of the student, heart stickers

Directions

1 With the student's help, cut one of the paper plates into a rounded heart shape. Just cut the top of the plate to make two humps, and leave the bottom of the heart round.
2 Cut the second plate in half down the center to make a semicircle.
3 Place the two plates together facing each other. The semicircular plate should match against the bottom of the rounded heart plate to make the heart pocket.
4 While the student holds the plates together, use the hole punch to make holes 1 inch apart along the outside edge where the plates touch.
5 Wrap some tape along the end of the piece of yarn to make a "needle." Thread the yarn through the holes to stick the heart pocket together. Tie or tape the ends in place.
6 Let the student decorate the heart with markers (and stickers if you have them). Write "Jesus loves the little children" on the heart.
7 Cut pictures of children from the magazines (and the student's photo if you have it) and stuff them into the heart.

Prayer Activity

. . . .

Give a Blessing

Formal blessings are sometimes performed in church services by priests, pastors and deacons. But informal blessings can be done by anyone. Help your child to come up with a blessing for those in the family—for her siblings and other family members.
Suggested blessings:

- "God loves you very much." (John 3:16)
- "May God give you peace." (Numbers 6:26)
- "God will give you everything you need." (Matthew 6:32–33; I Timothy 6:17)

The child can lay a hand on the person's shoulder or back and say a simple blessing. Additionally, have your child ask you for a blessing, and you place your hand on her shoulder and offer a blessing.

Memory Work

. . . .

Review the Books of the New Testament

Directions

Say to the student: "Let's review all the books of the New Testament that you've learned so far. Remember, the first five books you learned were Matthew, Mark, Luke, John, and Acts. Let's chant those together three times."

(Together, three times): Matthew, Mark, Luke, John, Acts.

Say, "Then we learned about the letters that one of Jesus' messengers, named Paul, sent to

Lesson 11: Jesus Blesses and Prays for the Children

different groups of Christians. There were nine of them: Romans, First and Second Corinthians, Galatians, Ephesians, Philippians, Colossians, First and Second Thessalonians. Let's chant those together three times."

(Together, three times): Romans, First and Second Corinthians, Galatians, Ephesians, Philippians, Colossians, First and Second Thessalonians.

Say, "Now let's say all of those together."

(Together): Matthew, Mark, Luke, John, Acts, Romans, First and Second Corinthians, Galatians, Ephesians, Philippians, Colossians, First and Second Thessalonians.

Coloring Page
· ·
Jesus Blesses the Little Children
Jesus cared about little children. He wasn't too busy to pray for them.

A Blessing

The Lord bless you and keep you.
The Lord make His face shine upon you
and be gracious to you.
The Lord turn His face toward you
and give you peace.

Numbers 6: 24-26

Christ and the Children by Carl Bloch

Used by permission of Hope Gallery, Salt Lake City, UT   www.hopegallery.com

Matthew 19:13–15

Matthew 19:13-15

Lesson 12: Jesus Is the Light of the World

Activities

Cooking Project: **"Light of the World" Stained-glass Cookies**
Craft Project: **Make a "Light of the World" Lantern**
Learning Game: **Light and Dark**
Science Activity: **Polar Night**
Memory Work: **Review the Books of the New Testament**
Coloring Page: **The Sun Rises After a Long, Dark Night**

Cooking Project
. . . .
"Light of the World" Stained-glass Cookies

You can use a sugar-cookie mix or the recipe below.

Ingredients

- ⅔ c. butter, softened
- ¾ c. sugar
- 1 tsp. baking powder
- ¼ tsp. salt
- 1 egg
- 1 tsp. vanilla extract
- 2 c. flour
- Nonstick cooking spray
- Assorted Jolly Ranchers or Fruit Life Savers (about 4 oz.)
- Also needed: large round cookie cutter or biscuit cutter, aluminum foil, sharp knife, 2 sandwich baggies, and a hammer

Directions

1   Beat the butter with an electric mixer. Let the student help you add the sugar, baking powder, and salt. Beat well.
2   With the student's help, beat in the egg and vanilla extract.
3   Add flour gradually—beat in as much as you can and then stir in the rest.

4   Divide the dough in half. (If it is a warm or humid day, you may need to chill the dough for a few hours to make it easier to work with.)
5   Roll out half the dough on a floured surface. The student should help you cut out the large circles with the cookie cutter and place them on a foil-lined baking sheet (spray the foil with nonstick cooking spray). With a sharp knife, cut a rectangle (candle) in the center of each cookie with a tear shape (flame) overtop (these two shapes should not connect). Remove the dough from the cut outs.
6   Repeat Step 5 with the remaining dough. Preheat oven to 375 degrees F.
7   Ask the student to sort the Jolly Ranchers by color (red, yellow, and blue are good choices). Unwrap them; place the yellow and red pieces into one sandwich baggie, and the blue candies into another.
8   Crush the contents of both bags with a hammer.
9   Have the student sprinkle the red and yellow pieces in the flame cutout and the blue in the candle cutout.
10 Bake at 375 degrees F. for 7–8 minutes or until the edges of the cookie are light brown. Let the cookies cool completely on the foil before you remove them.

Craft Project

Make a "Light of the World" Lantern

Materials

- 1 clean glass jar, any size (e.g., Mason jar, pickle jar, mayonnaise jar)
- Bottle of school glue
- Construction paper, preferably darker colors (red, dark green or blue) rather than light colors
- Scissors
- Pencil
- Tea light, votive candle, or glow stick

Directions

1   Cut the construction paper to be the same height as the jar.
2   The instructor should write "JESUS" in large block letters on the construction paper. The letters should be as tall as possible, but the word can be no longer than the circumference of the jar.
3   The student should cut out the letters.
4   Now have the student glue the paper to the jar. You should be able to see into the interior of the jar where the letters J-E-S-U-S were cut out.
5   Let the glue dry. Have the student put the candle or the glow stick inside the jar to light it up. A candle lantern makes a wonderful table centerpiece. A glow-stick lantern is great to put on a bedside table at night. Say to the student, "Whenever you look at the lantern, remember that Jesus is the light of the world."

Light and Dark

Directions

1. Darken the room or blindfold the child. Have a variety of objects for the child to feel and identify. It is best to make them a little tricky. Have the child try to describe each object he is feeling. After the child guesses what it might be, take off the blindfold (or turn on the lights) and have him describe it again while he is looking at it. Ask him if the objects were easier to understand and identify in the dark or in the light.

2. If you are at home, try having the child do ordinary tasks without being able to see. For instance, you could blindfold your child and have him try to put toothpaste on his toothbrush and brush his teeth. Or blindfold him before he tries to eat breakfast or before he writes his name or a short sentence. (Yes, some of these tasks will get a little messy since the child can't see what he's doing. That is part of the point, and part of the fun.) Ask him if these things were harder than what he is used to.

3. After these activities say, "Was it simpler to do these things in the dark or in the light?" He will probably answer "In the light." Remind him, from this week's lesson, that Jesus is the light who shows us what God is like and what we are supposed to do.

Science Activity

Polar Night

As we learned in the lesson, the Arctic Circle experiences polar night (24 hours of darkness) at the winter solstice. This activity shows the student why this happens. Do this activity at night or in a room with little or no light. Start the activity with the room light on.

Materials

- Globe with lines of latitude
- Lamp with the shade removed (or other small, intense light source)
- Small stickers plus 1 medium-size sticker

Directions

1. Say to the student, "This is a globe, a map of the whole world. It is round because the world is round like a ball. The Arctic Circle is a region of the earth above a certain latitude (66 degrees north of the Equator). That means it's the area near the 'top'! Find this area on the globe and put small stickers along the latitude line." (See illustration to the right).

2   Say, "You will see parts of Alaska, Russia, Greenland, Norway, Sweden, Iceland, and Canada rest within the Arctic Circle. The Arctic Ocean is also in the Arctic Circle." (Show the student the Arctic Ocean.) Say, "Why is it called a circle? If you look at it from the top of the globe, you will see that it does form a circle around the top of the earth." Show the student the globe from the top to help him see the Arctic Circle from above.

3   Say, "The earth spins along an axis, an imaginary line that runs through the center of the earth. Imagine a spinning top—it spins around its center axis, which is vertical (or straight up and down). The earth spins like a top, but it is tilted just a little bit to the side. Spin the globe. Do you see how it spins? Do you see where the metal pole attaches to the top of the globe? Do you see how it is tilted off to the side a little bit? That shows where the earth's axis is (we call this location at the top of the earth the North Pole)."

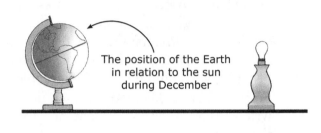

The position of the Earth in relation to the sun during December

4   Say, "Because of the slight tilt of the earth on its axis, the Arctic Circle sometimes has a whole day and night where it is completely dark. The sun never shines directly on the Arctic Circle in December. Let's see how this works."

5   Put the lamp in the center of the room and turn it on. Say, "This lamp will be the sun. Now let's turn off the rest of the lights." Put the globe a few feet back from the lamp.

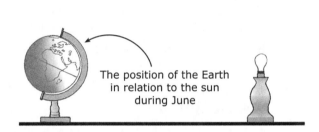

The position of the Earth in relation to the sun during June

6   Make sure the metal arc that holds the globe's axis is positioned as far away as possible from the lamp. (The North Pole will be facing away from the lamp; see "December" diagram.) Say, "This is where the earth is positioned in December. Spin the globe while keeping it on that spot of the floor. The earth takes 24 hours to spin around once. Put one big sticker on the middle of Greenland (remember, Greenland is inside the Arctic Circle). Spin the globe again and watch the sticker. Do you see how it is always dark in Greenland during December? During December, the Arctic Circle is in complete darkness for 24 hours—that is called polar night. This is the kind of darkness the lesson was talking about."

7   Say, "The earth travels in a circle around the sun." Make a mental note of something in your room (an object or corner that is up high) towards which the top of the metal arc (the North Pole) is pointing. Pick up the globe and walk counterclockwise in a circle around the lamp, keeping the North Pole pointing at that same object or corner. Say, "It takes one year for the earth to go all the way around the sun." Now go back to where you were in "December." Then walk one half of the way around the circle, so you are standing in the spot where the earth is in June. The North Pole should now be facing towards the lamp; see "June" diagram.

8   Have the student spin the globe in this new spot in the room, and watch the sticker on Greenland. Ask, "Is it in the light or the dark? Is it ever in the dark when it spins?" Tell the student that during June, there are 24 hours of daylight—this is called polar day, because it only happens around the North and South poles.

                                                 Lesson 12: Jesus Is the Light of the World

Memory Work

Review the Books of the New Testament

Directions

Say to the student: "Let's review all the books of the New Testament that you've learned so far. Remember, the first five books you learned were Matthew, Mark, Luke, John, and Acts. Let's chant those together three times."

(Together, three times): Matthew, Mark, Luke, John, Acts.

Say, "Then we learned about the letters that one of Jesus' messengers, named Paul, sent to different groups of Christians. There were nine of them: Romans, First and Second Corinthians, Galatians, Ephesians, Philippians, Colossians, First and Second Thessalonians. Let's chant those together three times."

(Together, three times): Romans, First and Second Corinthians, Galatians, Ephesians, Philippians, Colossians, First and Second Thessalonians.

Say, "Now let's say all of those together."

(Together): Matthew, Mark, Luke, John, Acts, Romans, First and Second Corinthians, Galatians, Ephesians, Philippians, Colossians, First and Second Thessalonians.

Coloring Page

The Sun Rises After a Long, Dark Night

In today's lesson, Jesus talked about light and darkness. Have you ever seen the sun rise? Have you seen the way it lights up everything that was dark before? In this picture, the sun is rising in the Arctic, in the northern part of the world, after weeks where there has been mostly only darkness.

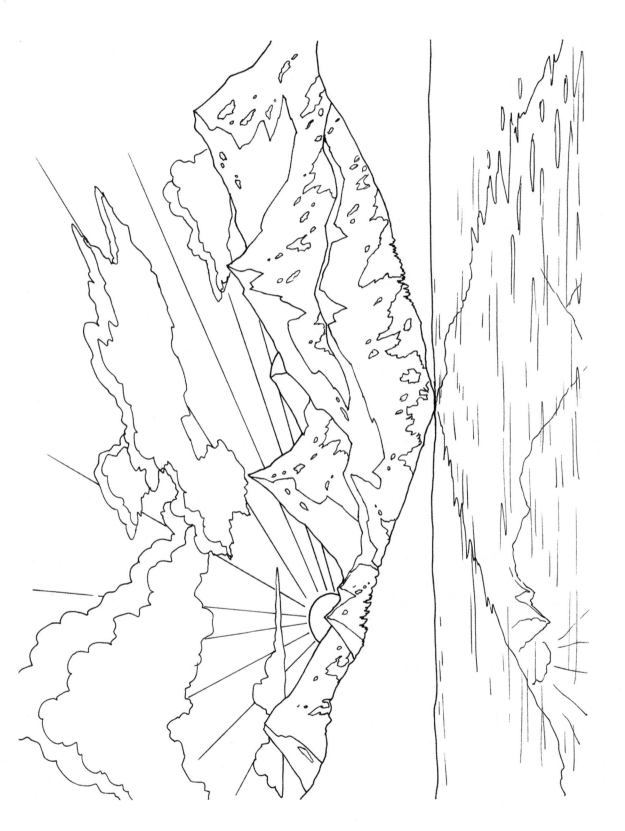

John 8:12

Lesson 13: Jesus Means Business

Activities

Science Activity: **Build a Bird's Nest**
Craft Project: **Make a Play-dough Bird's Nest**
Memory Work: **Review the Books of the New Testament**
Coloring Page: **Foxes and Birds Have Their Homes**

Science Activity

• •

Build a Bird's Nest

"Foxes have holes and birds of the air have nests, but the Son of Man has no place to lay his head."
Build a bird's nest that a bird might actually use in the spring! Remind the student that even the
birds have a nest to rest in, but Jesus had little rest during his time on earth.

Materials

- Mud
- Spade or shovel
- Bucket
- Brown paper lunch bag
- Nest-making supplies: twigs, grass, leaves, moss, straw, yarn, fabric scraps, cotton balls, dryer lint
- Newspaper or plastic tablecloth to cover the work surface (or better yet, do this outside)
- Rubber or latex gloves (if you want to keep your hands clean)

Directions

1 Send the student outside to dig up some mud with the shovel and put it in the bucket. If the ground is dry, dig up dirt and add water to get mud.
2 Roll down the top of the paper lunch bag (imagine you are cuffing a pant leg) until the lunch bag is about ⅓ of its original size.
3 Cover the work surface or do this activity on the ground outside. Scoop some mud into the paper bag and smooth it up the sides of the bag to coat the entire inside. Stick in any fortifying materials (twigs, grass, leaves, straw, string, fabric).
4 Coat with another layer of mud. Make sure to leave a round hollow inside the nest so the bird has a place to sit. Add more fortifying materials and more mud until the nest is strong.

5 Gather soft materials (fabric, moss, fluffed-up cotton balls, dryer lint, etc.) and line the inside of the nest. Let the nest dry for a day.

6 OPTIONAL: If it is nesting season in the area where you live (generally in the spring if you live in a temperate climate, but almost year-round in tropical areas), find a spot in a tree and help the student carefully set the nest there. This is a basket nest, used mostly by North American songbirds. Keep checking the nest (especially if it is springtime) to see if any birds move in. Remind the student that birds can be very choosy about where they nest, so they might not use yours . . . but they might!

Craft Project

• •

Make a Play-dough Bird's Nest

This activity is like the first one, but these nests are just for display. Use purchased brown and blue play dough, or make your own salt dough using the recipe below.

Materials (for each student)

- Brown dough (about 1 c.)
- Blue dough (about ½ c.)
- Nest supplies: twigs, grass, straw, leaves, string

Directions

1 Have the student roll the brown dough into a ball and press her fingers into the center to create a nest/bowl shape.

2 Show her how to stick twigs, grass, straw, etc., into the nest to give it a realistic appearance.

3 Ask the student to roll the blue dough into small egg shapes, and then help her place them inside the nest.

SALT-DOUGH RECIPE

Ingredients

- 1 c. salt
- 1¼ c. warm water
- 3 c. flour
- Plastic bag
- OPTIONAL: Food coloring

Directions

1 In a large bowl, have the student mix together the salt with the warm water.

2 Gradually add the flour, enough to make a smooth (but not goopy) dough. Knead into a ball.

3 Knead in food coloring if desired, or you can paint the project at the very end. Make the dough green or brown (for brown, mix equal drops red, blue, and yellow).

4 The dough can be stored overnight in a plastic bag in the refrigerator.

Memory Work

. . . .

Review the Books of the New Testament

Directions

Say to the student: "Let's review all the books of the New Testament that you've learned so far. Remember, the first five books you learned were Matthew, Mark, Luke, John, and Acts. Let's chant those together three times."

(Together, three times): Matthew, Mark, Luke, John, Acts.

Say, "Then we learned about the letters that one of Jesus' messengers, named Paul, sent to different groups of Christians. There were nine of them: Romans, First and Second Corinthians, Galatians, Ephesians, Philippians, Colossians, First and Second Thessalonians. Let's chant those together three times."

(Together, three times): Romans, First and Second Corinthians, Galatians, Ephesians, Philippians, Colossians, First and Second Thessalonians.

Say, "Now let's say all of those together."

(Together): Matthew, Mark, Luke, John, Acts, Romans, First and Second Corinthians, Galatians, Ephesians, Philippians, Colossians, First and Second Thessalonians.

Coloring Page

. . . .

Foxes and Birds Have Their Homes

Jesus had to travel around teaching and healing people, so he didn't get to have a home of his own. He said that even the birds and foxes had homes, but that he did not. The bird in this picture, the European roller (which lives not only in Europe but also in the Middle East, where Jesus lived) makes its homes in holes in trees and cliffs. It is brightly colored in blue and orange. The red fox shown here is orange-ish red in color and likes to live in dens, as Jesus said in today's verse.

Matthew 8:18–22

Lesson 14: Jesus Gives Rest to the Weary

Activities

Craft Project: **Make an Ox Yoke**
History Project: **Make the Ten Commandments Tablets**
Memory Work: **Review the Books of the New Testament**
Coloring Page: **Oxen with a Yoke**

Craft Project

. . . .

Make an Ox Yoke

Make a yoke so the student understands what Jesus is referencing.

Materials

- Yoke template (Student Page 137)
- Marker
- Corrugated cardboard, approx. 8" x 11" (a piece of a larger cardboard box would work)
- Scissors
- Brown paint
- Paintbrush
- Twine (about 2 feet long)
- Plastic ring from the bottom of a soda or water bottle cap
- Craft glue

Directions

1 Have the student help you cut out the yoke template on Student Page 137.
2 Using the marker, let the student trace the yoke template onto the cardboard to make two cardboard yokes. Cut those two yokes out.
3 Cut the twine into three pieces: two 8-inch pieces and one 4-inch piece.
4 Tie the 4-inch piece to the plastic circle, so that

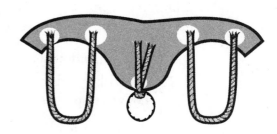

the circle is in the center of the twine piece. Have the student help you glue the ends of the 4-inch piece of twine to the center of one of the yoke cardboard cutouts (this side will now be the "inside" or "back"; see illustration of yoke in progress on page 133).

5 Tie a thick knot at both ends of each of the 8-inch pieces of twine.

6 Bend each 8-inch piece of twine in half, forming a U-shape, and glue the ends to the same side of the same piece of cardboard yoke as the 4-inch twine (see illustration on page 133).

7 Let the student spread glue over the rest of the cardboard yoke piece that has the strings (just the side facing up with the strings). Set the other cardboard yoke piece on top of it so that the two pieces exactly overlap. Press to seal. Let dry.

8 Have the student paint the yoke brown, to resemble wood. Let dry. Say, "Each ox would put its head through a loop. They were linked together by the wooden yoke. The center circle is there so a rope can be tied from the yoke to the plow that the oxen pull."

History Project

. . . .

Make the Ten Commandments Tablets

On Mount Sinai, the Lord gave Moses ten commandments carved on two stone tablets. These commandments told people how they should live. By the time of Jesus, some of the religious leaders had added more rules, which weighed the people down and were hard to follow. Here we are going to look at the original ten.

Materials

- Coffee dough OR sawdust dough (see recipes at bottom of this activity)
- Rolling pin
- Knife (plastic disposable one is fine)
- Wooden skewer with pointed end (such as the skewers used for shish kebabs)
- Large cookie sheet (although you may find it easier to use 2 cookie sheets)

Directions

1 Mix the dough according to the directions. Divide the dough in half. Have the student help you roll out each piece onto the cookie sheet until it is a rectangle ¼ to ½ inch thick.

2 Using the knife, trim each piece into a tablet shape (a rectangle with a rounded top).

3 Using the wooden skewer, have the student carve the numerals 1 through 10 into the tablets. (These numbers will represent the text of the commandments; most children this age are not yet able to carve or write so much text. If your child is ready to write/carve lengthier text, here is an abbreviated version, or you can find the full text in Exodus 20: 2–17). Different Christian denominations divide the commandments in different ways, so you may wish to copy the list your church uses.

> **The Ten Commandments**
> 1. Have no other gods before Me.
> 2. Do not worship idols.

3. Do not wrongly use the name of God.
4. Keep the Sabbath holy.
5. Honor your parents.
6. Do not murder.
7. Do not commit adultery.
8. Do not steal.
9. Do not lie.
10. Do not covet what belongs to other people.

4 Let the tablets dry. You can air dry them (this will take a while) or bake them at 350 degrees F, checking on them every 15 minutes to see if they are dry.

COFFEE-DOUGH RECIPE

Ingredients

- 3 c. flour
- 1½ c. salt
- 3 c. used coffee grounds
- 1½ c. cold coffee
- Flour to put on the surface where you'll do your kneading

Directions

1 Mix flour, salt, used coffee grounds, and cold coffee.
2 Knead on floured surface until smooth.

SAWDUST-DOUGH RECIPE

Ingredients

- 3 c. sawdust (You can get free sawdust from the wood-cutting area at a home improvement store.)
- 1½ c. flour
- ¾ c. water
- 3 Tbsp. white glue
- Extra flour to put on kneading surface

Directions

1 Shake sawdust through a sieve to remove any splinters or wood bits.
2 Mix sifted sawdust, flour, water, and white glue.
3 Knead on a flour surface until smooth.

Memory Work

. . . .

Review the Books of the New Testament

Directions

Say to the student: "Let's review all the books of the New Testament that you've learned so far. Remember, the first five books you learned were Matthew, Mark, Luke, John, and Acts. Let's chant those together three times."

(Together, three times): Matthew, Mark, Luke, John, Acts.

Say, "Then we learned about the letters that one of Jesus' messengers, named Paul, sent to different groups of Christians. There were nine of them: Romans, First and Second Corinthians, Galatians, Ephesians, Philippians, Colossians, First and Second Thessalonians. Let's chant those together three times."

(Together, three times): Romans, First and Second Corinthians, Galatians, Ephesians, Philippians, Colossians, First and Second Thessalonians.

Say, "Now let's say all of those together."

(Together): Matthew, Mark, Luke, John, Acts, Romans, First and Second Corinthians, Galatians, Ephesians, Philippians, Colossians, First and Second Thessalonians.

Coloring Page

. . . .

Oxen with a Yoke

These oxen are wearing a yoke that keeps them going in the right direction while they work. Some religious leaders were weighing the people down with lots of extra things to do, to be sure they were keeping God's rules. But Jesus said the only "yoke" people needed to have, to stay in the right path, was to follow his teaching. He doesn't give us lots of extra tasks to weigh us down.

Yoke Template

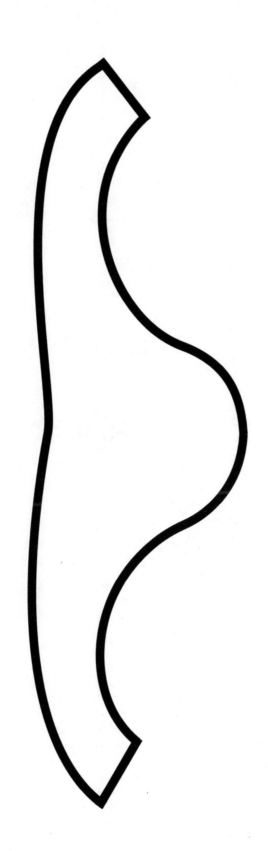

Matthew 11:28–30

Lesson 15: Jesus' Mother and Brothers

Activities

Craft Project: **A Family Album**
Craft Project: **Make Jesus' Family Tree**
Memory Work: **Review the Books of the New Testament**
Coloring Page: **We Can Be Part of Jesus' Family**

Craft Project
. . . .
A Family Album

All those who follow Jesus, no matter who they are or where they live, are part of the same family. Make a photo album of the student's brothers and sisters in Christ.

Materials

- Small photo album (you can find these at a dollar store)
- Pictures of Christians from around the world (try finding them at websites of missionary groups, or in your denomination's magazine or newsletter, or missionary photos from your church)
- Pictures of Christians from other eras of history (try www.christianhistory.net, and you can also use pictures of Jesus' followers from the coloring pages in this book)
- Small piece of paper (the size of a photograph)
- Crayons or markers

Directions

1 On the piece of paper, help the student write "God is my father. Jesus is my brother. We are all family in Christ." She may embellish it with pictures and designs.
2 Slide it into the cover of the album, if possible, or on the first album page.
3 Help the student cut out pictures of other people who follow Jesus.
4 Let the student slide the photographs of her Christian family into the sleeve pages of the album. Remind the student that if we love and follow Jesus, we become a part of his family. All the people who love and follow Jesus are like brothers and sisters in the same family.

Craft Project

• •

Make Jesus' Family Tree

This project is most fun to do with real leaves (use fresh, not dried, as they are easier to write on), but you can use cut-out paper leaves if real ones aren't available.

Materials (for each student)

- Assorted leaves (if you have time, give the student a bag and let her go outside and gather these herself)
- ½ piece of brown construction paper
- 1 piece of plain white paper
- Dark marker or pen
- Glue stick

Directions

1   Cut the brown construction paper into the shape of a tree trunk.
2   Lay the white paper down (in "portrait" orientation) and glue the tree trunk to it. The trunk should start at the bottom of the paper and extend to the middle of the paper.
3   Write "Jesus' Family Tree" at the top of the white paper.
4   Now turn the leaves smooth side up, and let the student write the names of fellow Christians on each leaf. This may include people who (as this week's lesson reminds us) listen to Jesus, love him, and try to do what he says. She should write her own name, your name, the name of her pastor or other Christians from your church or neighborhood or school, etc.
5   Now rub the glue stick on the back of each leaf and glue it to the paper to make a tree. Feel free to overlap the leaves, but do your best to leave the names visible.
6   Remind the student that Jesus said that whoever listened to and obeyed God was a member of his family.

Memory Work

• •

Review the Books of the New Testament

Directions

Say to the student: "Let's review all the books of the New Testament that you've learned so far. Remember, the first five books you learned were Matthew, Mark, Luke, John, and Acts. Let's chant those together three times."

(Together, three times): Matthew, Mark, Luke, John, Acts.

Say, "Then we learned about the letters that one of Jesus' messengers, named Paul, sent to different groups of Christians. There were nine of them: Romans, First and Second Corinthians, Galatians, Ephesians, Philippians, Colossians, First and Second Thessalonians. Let's chant those together three times."

(Together, three times): Romans, First and Second Corinthians, Galatians, Ephesians, Philippians, Colossians, First and Second Thessalonians.

Say, "Now let's say all of those together."

(Together): Matthew, Mark, Luke, John, Acts, Romans, First and Second Corinthians, Galatians, Ephesians, Philippians, Colossians, First and Second Thessalonians.

Coloring Page

We Can Be Part of Jesus' Family

Jesus said that all of his followers can be as close to him as his mother and his brothers. If they love him and follow what he says, they will become part of his family. And if we love and follow Jesus, *we* become part of his family as well.

Luke 8:19–21

Unit 4

The Sermon on the Mount

Lesson 16: Salt and Light

Activities

Science Activity: **Grow Salt Crystals**
Science Activity: **Salt and Soda Overflow**
Cooking Project: **Make Your Own Pickles**
Craft Project: **Salt of the Earth Picture**
Memory Work: **Review the Books of the New Testament**
Coloring Page: **A City on a Hill**

Science Activity
. . . .
Grow Salt Crystals

Materials

- 1 c. water
- ¼ c. salt (a little more may be needed)
- Small saucepan
- Clear jar (without lid)
- 1 small piece cardboard
- Spoon
- OPTIONAL: Food coloring, any color

Directions

1 The instructor should boil the water in the saucepan on the stove. Gradually add the salt a little bit at a time. After each addition, stir the water until the salt dissolves. Keep adding salt until the salt no longer dissolves when you stir it.
2 Remove the pan from heat. Carefully pour the water into the clear jar for the student.
3 Being careful not to touch the hot water, the student can place the cardboard into the liquid and push it to the bottom of the jar with the spoon. He may add a few drops of food coloring to the jar, if desired (this will give you colored crystals).
4 Set the jar in a sunny spot for several days. As the water evaporates, salt crystals will form and cling to the cardboard.

Science Activity

Salt and Soda Overflow

Materials

- 26 oz. canister of table salt with a pour spout
- 1 can of cola
- Baking pan (to catch the overflow)

Directions

1 Have the student open the can of cola and drink or pour out a little bit.
2 Place the can on the baking pan.
3 Help the student open the spout to the salt canister.
4 Quickly pour a few tablespoons of salt into the cola (no need to measure, just pour salt into the can for a second or two).
5 Watch the cola overflow everywhere!
6 Say, "See how the salt has affected the cola? In today's lesson, Jesus talked about how people who follow him will have an effect on those around them. They'll make the world different, and better, just by following Jesus' teachings."

Why does this happen? In a can of soda, carbon dioxide gas is trapped inside the water. If you add salt, the salt breaks up the surface tension of the water (the tendency of water molecules to want to stick together), and the carbon dioxide bubbles are all freed up to cling to the salt crystals. All of those bubbles coming free at once makes a large amount of fizz—too much for the soda can to hold.

Cooking Project

Make Your Own Pickles

This recipe does not involve canning. The cucumbers sit in a brine solution for six weeks. Yes, this activity takes a while, but the actual work is minimal and children will enjoy seeing the preservative value of salt in action.

Ingredients

- 2½ lbs. pickling cucumbers (you can also pickle the same weight of green beans if you prefer)
- 2½ c. of salt (you may need an additional cup)
- 2 quarts of water (you may need an additional 2 c.)
- 2 Large pots or bowls
- Stoneware plate that fits inside pot
- Kitchen towel
- Cider vinegar (you will use this at the end of the pickling process)
- 1 c. sugar (you will use this at the end of the pickling process)

Directions

1 Have the student wash the vegetables. If the cucumbers are small, leave them whole. If they are large, have the student cut them into spears. If green beans are being used instead of cucumbers, have the student trim them and cut them to the appropriate length.

2 Help the student make the brine solution. Have him pour 2 quarts of water into a large pot and add 1 cup of salt (the remaining salt will be used through the next six weeks). Heat and stir until salt is dissolved.

3 Have the student put the vegetables into a large bowl or pot. Have him pour the brine solution over them. The vegetables should be completely submerged. If not, prepare another batch of brine solution as in step 2 and add that to the pot or bowl.

4 Put the plate into the pot, covering the vegetables, to weigh them down and keep them in the brine.

5 Cover the pot with a kitchen towel and store the pot in a cool, dark location overnight.

6 The next day, have the student remove the towel and pour ½ cup of salt on the plate. Do not stir the salt. This helps the salt release slowly and aids the brining process. Re-cover.

7 After a week, have the student add ⅛ of a cup of salt to the plate. The plate will become covered with salt crystals (this is normal). Keep reminding the student to add ⅛ of a cup of salt every week for the next 5 weeks.

8 It is important to remind the student to remove any scum that forms on the top of the brine solution throughout the six week process. This scum can spoil the vegetables if it isn't removed. Bubbles will form in the brine in about two weeks. This is a normal part of the fermentation process.

9 After six weeks, your vegetables are ready to eat! If you made the pickles, you can have the student drain them and put them in a container. Let the student pour cider vinegar and a cup of sugar over the pickles. Put a lid on the container and store them for up to 2 weeks. If you made the green beans, drain and rinse. Heat them in a saucepan with a little water until hot.

Craft Project

· ·

Salt of the Earth Picture

If you want to save time, skip coloring the salt with the chalk, and instead color the earth picture with blue and green marker and then apply regular salt.

Materials

- Earth picture (Student Page 153)
- 1 c. table salt
- 2 pieces of paper
- 9" x 13" baking dish
- Blue and green sidewalk chalk
- 2 bowls
- School glue
- Paintbrush

Directions

1 Put a piece of paper in the bottom of the baking dish.
2 Help the student pour half the salt onto the paper. Spread the salt over the paper.
3 Have the student rub the salt with the blue sidewalk chalk. The more he rubs, the bluer the salt will get.
4 Help the student carefully pick up the paper with the salt on it and dump the blue salt in a bowl.
5 Repeat steps 1–4 with the other half of the salt and the green chalk and the second sheet of paper.
6 Put the picture of earth inside the baking dish. The student should dip the paintbrush in the glue and paint the gray parts of the earth (the water).
7 Dump the blue salt on the paper and spread it around so all the gluey parts are covered. The blue salt will stick to the glue, making the water parts of the world look blue.
8 Shake the excess blue salt back into the bowl.
9 Paint the white parts of the earth (the continents) with the glue.
10 Pour the green salt over the picture and spread it around so all the gluey parts are covered. Much of the green salt will stick to the glue.
11 Shake the excess salt back into its bowl.
12 Let picture dry.

Memory Work
· ·
Review the Books of the New Testament

Directions

Say to the student: "Let's review all the books of the New Testament that you've learned so far. Remember, the first five books you learned were Matthew, Mark, Luke, John, and Acts. Let's chant those together three times."

(Together, three times): Matthew, Mark, Luke, John, Acts.

Say, "Then we learned about the letters that one of Jesus' messengers, named Paul, sent to different groups of Christians. There were nine of them: Romans, First and Second Corinthians, Galatians, Ephesians, Philippians, Colossians, First and Second Thessalonians. Let's chant those together three times."

(Together, three times): Romans, First and Second Corinthians, Galatians, Ephesians, Philippians, Colossians, First and Second Thessalonians.

Say, "Now let's say all of those together."

(Together): Matthew, Mark, Luke, John, Acts, Romans, First and Second Corinthians, Galatians, Ephesians, Philippians, Colossians, First and Second Thessalonians.

Coloring Page

• •

A City on a Hill

In today's lesson, Jesus says that the people who love him and obey his words will show to others what God is like. They'll be like a bright city that can be seen for miles around.

Salt of the Earth

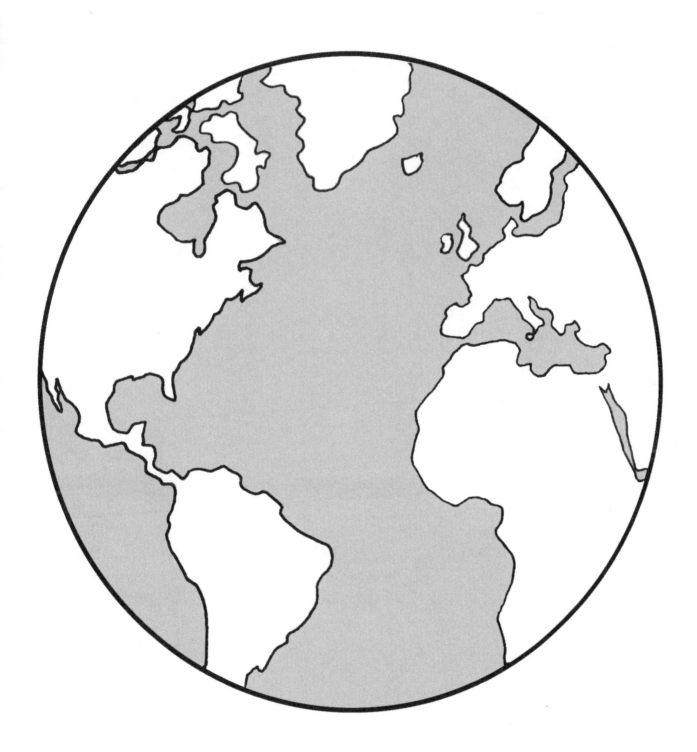

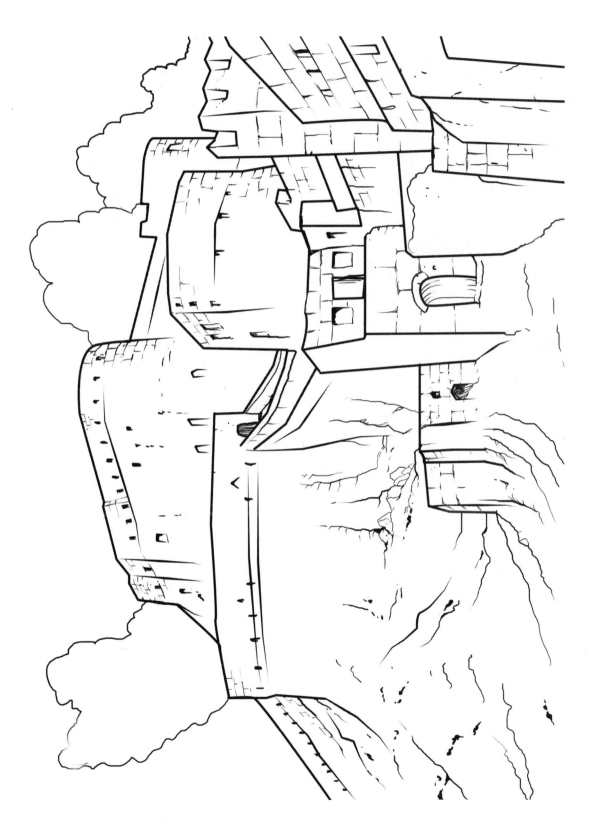

Matthew 5:13–16

Lesson 17: Just Be Truthful

Activities

Game Activity: **Oath Red Light/Green Light**
Craft Project: **Just Tell the Truth**
Game Activity: **"Cheat"**
Memory Work: **The Books of the New Testament, Part III**
Coloring Page: **Telling the Truth**

Game Activity
. . . .
Oath Red Light/Green Light

This game will help remind the student of what an oath is: a promise in God's name. It uses Old Testament verses that talk about oaths and solemn promises. You will need at least 3 players for this game (one to be the caller, two to race). It's best to play this outside where the students have plenty of room to run.

Materials

- Bible Oaths (Student Page 161)
- At least three players

Directions

1 Tear out Student Page 161.
2 Have the caller stand thirty to forty feet away from the runners. If the students aren't yet able to read large chunks of text, then you, the instructor, should be the caller.
3 Tell the runners that an oath is a very important promise. Tell them to listen carefully while the caller reads the verses from the Bible Oaths, listening for the important word, "oath."
4 Have the caller begin to read one of the verses from the Bible Oaths. When the caller gets to the word "oath," the runners should begin walking or running forward toward the caller as fast as they can (the word "oath" is the "green light").
5 When the caller starts reading the rest of the words in the verse, the runners must stop ("red light").

6   If the caller is a student, remind the caller that when she finishes each verse she should move on to the next. The caller may read the verses in any order, as many times as is necessary for the runners to reach the caller.

7   The first runner to reach the caller wins and becomes the caller for the next round.

Craft Project

. . . .

Just Tell the Truth

Materials

- Just Tell the Truth (Student Page 163)
- Crayons, markers, or colored pencils

Directions

1   Say to the student: "In today's lesson, Jesus taught that we should tell the truth all the time. We should not need to add anything to our words, to convince people that we are being honest and truthful."

2   Have the student tear out Student Page 163.

3   Help the student read the statements on the Student Page. Explain that each one of these is a way that people try to convince people that they are telling the truth.

4   If you or the student can think of other phrases that are used in this way in your house, add them to the Student Page. Decorate the page.

5   Hang the page in a place where you and the student will see it often (the refrigerator works well for this). This week, use this page as a memory aid, to help the student remember to "just tell the truth," without any additions.

Game Activity

. . . .

"Cheat"

This is a card game for three or more players. It is about lying and telling the truth.

Materials

- A deck of cards
- At least three players (if there are more than four people, you can play with two decks).

Directions

1   Split the deck(s) of cards up equally among all the players.

2   Start with the person to the dealer's right. That person has to play aces, however many she wants. But as she puts the card down, she must say what kind of card it is and how many of it she's putting down. So if she puts down three aces, she must say "Three aces."

3   The next person has to put down twos, the next person threes, and so on up to kings, after which it goes back down to aces.

4   The trick of this game is that you can lie about what you're putting down. Anyone can

put down, for example, a 4, a 7, and a 9 and say "three kings", or she can put down four cards and say she only put down three. Anyone can put down any wrong cards or any number of wrong cards, but if you think someone is cheating you say "cheat" before the next player's turn.

5   If she was cheating, she must pick up all the cards that have been played and add them to her hand. If she wasn't cheating, you have to take all the cards.

6   The first player to run out of cards wins.

Memory Work
• •
The Books of the New Testament, Part III

Materials

- New Testament Books, Part III (Student Page 165)

Directions

Say to the student: "We are going to learn some more New Testament books today. First, let's review the books we've learned so far. The first five were Matthew, Mark, Luke, John, and Acts. Let's say those together."

[Together]: Matthew, Mark, Luke, John, Acts.

"Then we learned nine more books, the letters that Paul wrote to different groups of people. They were Romans, First and Second Corinthians, Galatians, Ephesians, Philippians, Colossians, First and Second Thessalonians. Let's say those together."

[Together]: Romans, First and Second Corinthians, Galatians, Ephesians, Philippians, Colossians, First and Second Thessalonians.

"Today we will learn just four more books. These are letters too, but these letters were sent to specific people instead of groups. We name them after the people they're addressed to. They are First and Second Timothy, Titus, Philemon [say "fie-LEE-mun"]. I'll say those again, and this time, say each one after me. First and Second Timothy [student says, "First and Second Timothy"], Titus, Philemon.*

"Now let's say those together four times."

[Together, four times]: First and Second Timothy, Titus, Philemon.

"Now let's say all of the books we've learned so far."

[Together]: Matthew, Mark, Luke, John, Acts, Romans, First and Second Corinthians, Galatians, Ephesians, Philippians, Colossians, First and Second Thessalonians, First and Second Timothy, Titus, Philemon.

Have the student tear out Student Page 165. She can decorate the sheet, and you should put it on the refrigerator or some other visible spot, to remind you and the student to review.

• •

Telling the Truth

In today's lesson, Jesus told us to tell the truth. That is how people will be able to trust what we say.

Bible Oaths

Deuteronomy 6:13–14
Fear the LORD your God, serve him only and take your **oaths** in his name. Do not follow other gods, the gods of the peoples around you.

Numbers 30:2
When a man makes a vow to the LORD or takes an **oath** to obligate himself by a pledge, he must not break his word but must do everything he said.

Deuteronomy 10:20
Fear the LORD your God and serve him. Hold fast to him and take your **oaths** in his name.

Just Tell the Truth

Honest to God

I swear

Cross my heart

For real

I'M SERIOUS

I REALLY MEAN IT THIS TIME

New Testament Books, Part III

Matthew

Mark

Luke

John

Acts

Romans

First and Second Corinthians

Galatians

Ephesians

Philippians

Colossians

First and Second Thessalonians

First and Second Timothy

Titus

Philemon

Matthew 5:33–37

Lesson 18: An Eye for an Eye, and a Tooth for a Tooth

Activities

Game Activity: **Respond Jesus' Way**
Cooking Project: **Showing Kindness**
Memory Work: **Review the Books of the New Testament**
Coloring Page: **Doing Right When Someone Else Does Wrong**

Game Activity

• •

Respond Jesus' Way

This is a multiple-choice quiz, and it is best done orally. Ask the questions to the student and read the answers with expression. This will help keep the mood light, and it also gives you the chance to discuss any specific situations with the student. If you are doing this activity with a group, you might try dividing the questions among the students, asking each student one question.

Materials

- Respond Jesus' Way quiz (Student Page 173)

Directions

1 Read the questions and answers to the student, and have him choose the kind of response Jesus was talking about. As it says in the lesson, "Jesus is saying that when people do mean things to us, we should not fight back ourselves . . . Be the person who walks away from a fight—and does something kind instead."

2 Here are the answers: 1 c, 2 a, 3 b, 4 c, 5 a, 6 b.

Cooking Project

. . . .

Showing Kindness

In this week's lesson, Jesus taught us the new way of doing things in God's kingdom: showing kindness even to those who have not been kind to us. This can be an abstract concept for a child to grasp, so here's a practical (and tasty) way that he can show thoughtfulness.

Help your student pick someone who isn't a favorite friend. This shouldn't be a bully or a complete stranger, but neither should it be a close friend. Jesus said that we should show generosity to those who haven't repaid (or can't repay) us, not just to our close friends (Luke 14:12). Together, bake these brownies and deliver them to the person you choose.

Ingredients

- 1 stick of butter OR margarine
- 2 squares of unsweetened baking chocolate
- 1 c. sugar
- 2 eggs
- ¾ c. flour
- ¼ c. Nesquik chocolate powder
- 1 tsp. baking powder
- Nonstick cooking spray
- Square brownie pan
- OPTIONAL: 1 c. chocolate or peanut-butter chips

Directions

1 Say to the student: "In today's lesson, Jesus taught us to be kind to everyone, not just to our best friends or people who give us things. How do you feel when I make something just for you? Pretty good, right? Well today, we are going to do that together for someone else."
2 Preheat an oven to 350 degrees F. and spray the square brownie pan with nonstick spray.
3 Have the student put the stick of butter or margarine and the two squares of baking chocolate in a microwave-safe bowl and microwave them for one minute. The student can then beat the mixture with a wooden spoon until it is just a brown liquid.
4 Have the student mix in the cup of sugar and the two eggs, then mix again.
5 Have the student add the flour, chocolate powder, and baking powder, and stir it all until there are no dry ingredients visible.
6 OPTIONAL: If desired, have the student add chocolate or peanut-butter chips.
7 Have the student pour the batter out into the pan. Be sure to tilt the pan so that there is brownie mixture in all four corners.
8 Bake for 10 minutes, or until a knife inserted in the center comes out clean.
9 Together, deliver a plate of these brownies to the person. In preparation for the delivery, say to the student, "How do you think [name of person] is going to feel when we give him/her these? When we give good things to other people, we are doing for them the same kind of thing that God does for us. God gives us good things like family, and pets, and [insert something your child would be grateful for]."

Memory Work

· ·

Review the Books of the New Testament

Directions

Say to the student: "Let's review the New Testament books we've learned so far. The first five were Matthew, Mark, Luke, John, and Acts. Let's say those together."

[Together]: Matthew, Mark, Luke, John, Acts.

"Then we learned nine more books, the letters that Paul wrote to different groups of people. They were Romans, First and Second Corinthians, Galatians, Ephesians, Philippians, Colossians, First and Second Thessalonians. Let's say those together."

[Together]: Romans, First and Second Corinthians, Galatians, Ephesians, Philippians, Colossians, First and Second Thessalonians.

"Then we learned four more books, the letters that Paul wrote to certain people: First and Second Timothy, Titus, Philemon. Let's say those together three times."

[Together, three times]: First and Second Timothy, Titus, Philemon.

"Now let's say all of the books we've learned so far."

[Together]: Matthew, Mark, Luke, John, Acts, Romans, First and Second Corinthians, Galatians, Ephesians, Philippians, Colossians, First and Second Thessalonians, First and Second Timothy, Titus, Philemon.

Coloring Page

· ·

Doing Right When Someone Else Does Wrong

One of these girls is selfishly taking toys that aren't hers, but the other girl is not going to be unkind in return. She's going to be kind to the selfish girl anyway.

Respond Jesus' Way Quiz

Choose the best way to respond to each situation. Remember, Jesus wants us to respond with kindness when someone is mean or unfair.

1. You are reading a book when your older brother comes by and knocks it out of your hands and laughs. Do you . . . ?
   a. Jump on his back and tackle him to the floor.
   b. Start screaming about it.
   c. Calmly pick up your book and walk away, saying nothing.

2. You are at the park when a kid shoves you aside to get down the slide first. Do you . . . ?
   a. Offer to let him go in front of you next time.
   b. Go sit on a bench and grumble about it.
   c. Push him down the slide face-first so he ends up with a mouthful of wood chips.

3. You add the last piece to the tallest block tower you have ever created when your baby sister toddles over, knocks it down, and claps with glee. Do you . . . ?
   a. Scream at her to go away and quit messing things up.
   b. Turn it into a game and build more towers for her to knock down.
   c. Grab her favorite toy and smash it so she can see how it feels.

4. When your brother's friend comes for a visit, your dad says the friend can ride your bike (even though you were planning to use it). Do you . . . ?
   a. Run to your room and slam the door.
   b. Whine to your father, "It's not fair!"
   c. Give the friend your bike helmet to use as he rides your bike.

5. Your sister picks a fight with you, and your mother comes in and punishes both of you, even though it wasn't your fault (and she won't listen to what you have to say). Do you . . . ?
   a. Apologize to your sister and accept your punishment without comment.
   b. Interrupt your mom over and over until she listens to you.
   c. Flick your sister's ear when your mom's back is turned.

6. A kid on your sports team says you are a lousy player. Do you . . . ?
   a. Punch him in the nose and say, "Now who's lousy?"
   b. Compliment him on how well he plays.
   c. Ignore him on the field and never give him the ball.

Matthew 5:38-42

Lesson 19: One Day at a Time

Activities

Art History Project: **Impressionist Pencil Holder**
History Project: **First-century Clothing Paper Dolls**
Craft Project: **Make a Bouquet of Lilies**
Memory Work: **Review the Books of the New Testament**
Coloring Page: **Lilies and Birds**

Art History Project

• •

Impressionist Pencil Holder

Jesus said that God gives the flowers their beautiful colors and shapes. Although the "lilies" in this activity are water lilies and not the "lilies of the field" mentioned in the lesson, they are beautiful nonetheless, and they give the student a chance to try a new style of art. If you do the craft project of a lily bouquet (see page 179), you can place the stems in this container.

Materials

- 15.5 oz. aluminum can (from canned beans or other food; clean and dried, label removed, top discarded)
- Scissors
- School glue or glue stick
- Computer
- Drawing supplies: pastels (these are best), markers, colored pencils, or crayons
- Plain white Paper

Directions

1   Say to the student, "Claude Monet was born in France more than one hundred years ago. In his style of painting, called Impressionism, the artist paints an ordinary object or scene, but uses quick strokes of the paintbrush to show movement and light. He or she doesn't just try to show an object but also shows how the light hits that object or how it moves. For example, Monet's painting titled *Impression, Sunrise* may not look exactly like a photograph of a sunrise over the water. Instead, it shows the impression that Monet got from the movement of the water and the light." You can see this painting at: http://en.wikipedia. org/wiki/File:Claude_Monet,_Impression,_soleil_levant,_1872.jpg.

2 Say, "Now, let's look at his Impressionist painting of water lilies." Using the computer, show the child Monet's painting of water lilies at http://en.wikipedia.org/wiki/File:Claude_Monet_038.jpg. (This painting is one of a series; others can be found at the Metropolitan Museum of Art in New York or the Art Institute of Chicago). Say, "Monet painted water lilies often. He had a pond full of them near his house in France."

3 Point out to the student that Monet painted the picture to show reflections in the water. Ask, "Have you ever looked at water, like in a sink or a pool, and seen wavy reflections in it? Monet wanted people to see those reflections in his painting."

4 Cut out a strip from the paper, the same height as the aluminum can. Find your own reflective, wavy surface, such as a puddle, a pool, or the kitchen sink filled with water. (Note: always supervise children around pools.) Have the student look at this surface, and have her draw what she sees onto the paper strip, using the coloring supplies. Drawing in an Impressionist style is beyond the abilities of most young children (and adults!) so don't insist that her picture resemble the Monet painting.

5 Help the student use the glue to attach her drawing to the outside of the can. Let dry. Use the can to hold pencils or markers.

History Project

• •

First-century Clothing Paper Dolls

Jesus tells his followers not to worry about what they wear, but what did *people wear back then? Color these paper dolls and dress them to learn about clothing in Israel in the time of Jesus.*

Materials

- Paper dolls and clothes (Student Pages 181, 183, and 185)
- Scissors
- Crayons, markers, or colored pencils

Directions

1 Have the student cut out the male and female paper dolls on Student Page 181. Both figures are in their undergarments (what they wear beneath their clothes). Let the student color the clothes in. Both figures are wearing simple leather sandals, the common shoes of the day (although the poor often went barefoot).

2 While the student is working on the figures, tell her, "Clothes were expensive back in Jesus' day, and many poor people had only one set of clothes. The basic item of clothing was a tunic. It was usually stitched from two pieces of cloth. Imagine that you have a long pillowcase. You would cut a V-shape in the top (closed end) of the pillowcase for your head, and cut a slit on each top corner to stick your arms through. That's just what a tunic was like—a giant sack with armholes and a V-shaped neck hole. A tunic could be made from wool, linen, or cotton. Men's tunics were usually short; women's tunics were usually long. The tunic was held in place by a girdle, which is like a belt made of leather or cloth. Look at Student Page 183. You will see a woman's basic tunic and a man's tunic. Color the woman's tunic (women's tunics were often blue). The man's tunic is tucked up into his girdle. If a man needed the freedom to work or run, he would gather up the bottom on his tunic and slide it up and under his girdle. Color this in. Cut out the tunics and

place them on the paper dolls."

3   Say, "To protect themselves from the heat of the sun, men and women covered their heads. Women wore a square of cloth over their heads to protect their neck and shoulders. They could move it farther forward to keep the sun out of their faces." Have the student color, cut out, and attach the head covering to the female paper doll. Tell the student, "Men wore a cap. This cap has material that flows outward to cover the man's neck and shoulders. These could be dyed blue, yellow, brown, or other colors."

4   Have the student color, cut out, and attach the cap to the male paper doll.

5   Say, "Look at your paper dolls. They are dressed like typical working people of the day. But what would they wear if they were rich? Remove the clothing from both paper dolls. Look at the clothes on Student Page 185, the wealthy people's clothing. You will see that both the male and female outfits have a tunic, but they each also have a cloak. A cloak is worn over the tunic. It can be made with an opening down the front (so it looks like a dressy bathrobe). Color in the man's outfit. A rich man would have had bright colors in his clothes—maybe even purple, which was very expensive to put into clothing." Point out to the student that this man's cloak has extra fringe along the bottom.

6   Say, "A cloak can also be made without an opening in the front. Imagine taking a long and wide scarf and cutting a hole in the middle of it for your head. One end of the scarf falls over your front while the other half covers your back. Notice that the woman's cloak is this style." Have the student color in the woman's outfit—again, use bright colors to show her wealth, not plain colors such as brown. Cut out and attach these outfits to the paper dolls.

7   Have the student color in the man's hat. This hat looks like a turban. The woman's head covering has extra detail work—and she is wearing earrings. Color in the head coverings, cut them out, and attach them to the paper dolls.

Craft Project

• •

Make a Bouquet of Lilies

Materials (for each student)

- 1 sheet each of yellow and green construction paper
- 3 drinking straws
- Scissors
- Pencil
- Stapler

Directions

1   The student should trace three handprints onto the yellow construction paper. Cut them out.

2   Wrap the fingers of the hand cutouts around the pencil to curl them.

3   Roll each hand into a tube shape so the bottom of the tube is the palm of the hand and the curls go outwards (like petals). Staple the palm end to the tip of a drinking straw.

4   Help them student draw six leaves on the green construction paper and cut the leaves out.

5   Help the student staple two leaves to the bottom of each drinking straw.
6   Say, "Now you have a bunch of green and yellow lilies! Think of how beautiful the flowers in the fields and yards are. They don't have to worry and fret about being colorful; God just makes them that way. He cares for you even more than the lilies, so you don't need to worry about what you need, either."

Memory Work

Review the Books of the New Testament

Directions

Say to the student: "Let's review the New Testament books we've learned so far. The first five were Matthew, Mark, Luke, John, and Acts. Let's say those together."

[Together]: Matthew, Mark, Luke, John, Acts.

"Then we learned nine more books, the letters that Paul wrote to different groups of people. They were Romans, First and Second Corinthians, Galatians, Ephesians, Philippians, Colossians, First and Second Thessalonians. Let's say those together."

[Together]: Romans, First and Second Corinthians, Galatians, Ephesians, Philippians, Colossians, First and Second Thessalonians.

"Then we learned four more books, the letters that Paul wrote to certain people: First and Second Timothy, Titus, Philemon. Let's say those together three times."

[Together, three times]: First and Second Timothy, Titus, Philemon.

"Now let's say all of the books we've learned so far."

[Together]: Matthew, Mark, Luke, John, Acts, Romans, First and Second Corinthians, Galatians, Ephesians, Philippians, Colossians, First and Second Thessalonians, First and Second Timothy, Titus, Philemon.

Coloring Page

Lilies and Birds

Jesus taught that God gives us all the things that we need. We don't need to be worried about where our food and clothes will come from. The bird in this picture is a Syrian woodpecker, which lives in the land where Jesus taught. You can color it red and black and white. The lilies in this picture, which are found in the part of the world where Jesus lived, are usually yellow and white (but you can also use other colors if you want!).

Paper Doll People

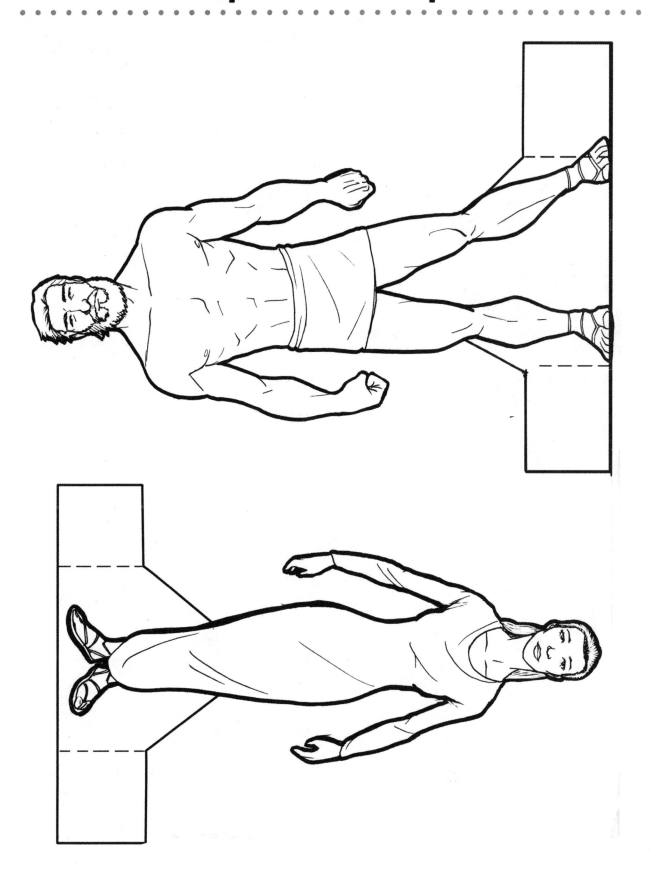

Clothing of Ordinary People

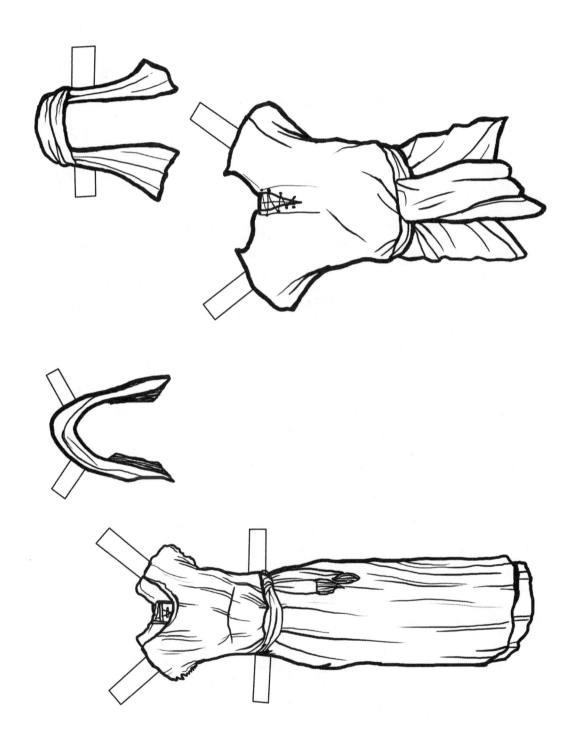

Clothing of Rich People

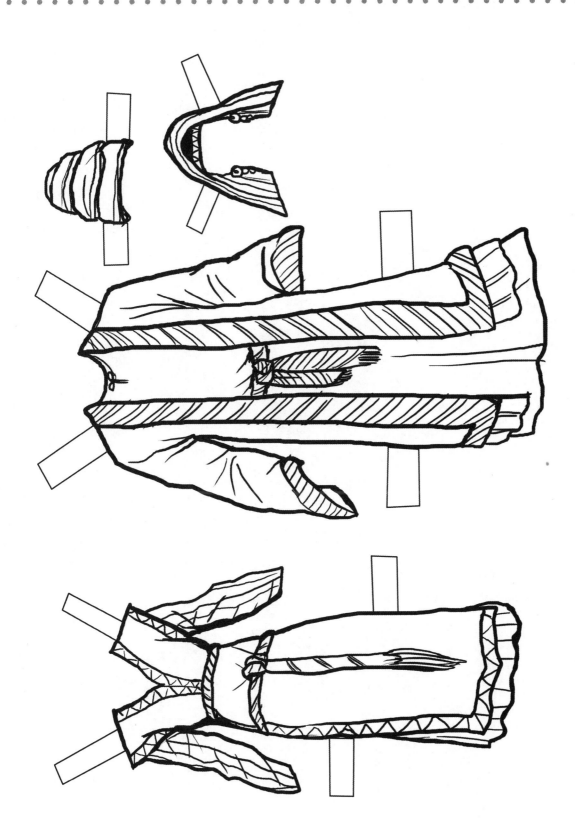

Matthew 6:25–34

Lesson 20: You Can Ask God Anything

Activities

Game Activity: **"Seek and Find" Word Search**
Game Activity: **"Ask and Receive" Go Fish**
Craft Project: **The Golden Rule**
Memory Work: **The Books of the New Testament, Part IV**
Coloring Page: **God Gives Us Good Things**

Game Activity

• •

"Seek and Find" Word Search

Materials

- "Seek and Find" Word Search (Student Page 193)
- Pencil

Directions

1 Tear out Student Page 193.
2 Say to the student, "Jesus said, 'Seek and you will find.' Look for the words from this week's lesson that are hidden in the word search. They can be written horizontally, vertically, or diagonally."
3 If needed, help the student find the words.
    Knock
    Door
    Open
    Seek
    Find
    Ask
    Given
    Son
    Bread
    Stone
    Fish
    Snake

Gifts
Children
Father
Law
Prophets

Game Activity

• •

"Ask and Receive" Go Fish

You will need 2–4 players for this game.

Materials

- Game cards (Student Pages 195, 197, 199, and 201)
- Scissors
- OPTIONAL: Coloring supplies

Directions

1 If the student would like to color the pictures on the game cards, do so now.
2 Cut out the cards.
3 Shuffle the cards, and deal out 5 cards to each player (if there are 2 players), 4 cards to each player (if there are 3 players), or 3 cards to each player (if there are 4 players). Place the remaining cards in a pile face-down between the players.
4 The players examine their cards and place down any matched pairs they have. Starting with the youngest player, this player may ask another player if he has the match to a card in the first player's hand. For example, if Player 1 has a stone, a father, and a fish, he may ask Player 2 OR Player 3 if he has a fish. Player 1 may not ask for a card that is not in his hand. If Player 2 (or 3) has the card, she hands it over to Player 1, who then places the match down on the table. If Player 2 (or 3) does not have the card, she says, "Go Fish," and Player 1 must choose a card from the face-down center pile.
5 Each player gets 1 turn, and then play continues clockwise. When a player runs out of cards, the game is over. The player with the most matched pairs at the end of the game wins.

Craft Project

• •

The Golden Rule

Materials (for each student)

- The Golden Rule (Student Page 203)
- School glue

Lesson 20: You Can Ask God Anything

- Gold glitter
- Disposable plate

Directions

1   Tell the student, "Tear out and look at look at Student Page 203. These words of Jesus are often called the Golden Rule because this is the most valuable rule in life. It sums up how God wants us to treat each other."
2   Help the student trace the words of the Golden Rule with the glue.
3   Let the student shake the gold glitter over the words and dump the excess glitter onto the plate.
4   Let dry. Hang up this golden verse to remind the student to do what it says.

Memory Work
• •
The Books of the New Testament, Part IV

Materials

- New Testament Books, Part IV (Student Page 205)

Directions

Say to the student: "Today we'll finish learning all the books of the New Testament. Let's review the New Testament books we've learned so far. The first five were Matthew, Mark, Luke, John, and Acts. Let's say those together."

[Together]: Matthew, Mark, Luke, John, Acts.

"Then we learned nine more books, the letters that Paul wrote to different groups of people. They were Romans, First and Second Corinthians, Galatians, Ephesians, Philippians, Colossians, First and Second Thessalonians. Let's say those together."

[Together]: Romans, First and Second Corinthians, Galatians, Ephesians, Philippians, Colossians, First and Second Thessalonians.

"Then we learned four more books, the letters Paul sent to specific people. Let's say those together."

[Together]: First and Second Timothy, Titus, Philemon.

"The last set of books we'll learn are also letters, written to different churches and people as messages by God, by different writers. Some were named after the people who wrote them, like James, Peter, John, and Jude. One was named after the people it was addressed to, and the last one, Revelation, is called that because it reveals, or shows, what God is doing and will do in the world. Here are the names of these letters: Hebrews, James, First and Second Peter, First, Second, and Third John, Jude, Revelation. I'll say those names again, and this time, say each one after me as I go. Hebrews *(student says 'Hebrews')*, James, First and Second Peter, First, Second, and Third John, Jude, Revelation."

"Now let's say those names together three times."

[Together, three times]: Hebrews, James, First and Second Peter, First, Second, and Third John, Jude, Revelation.

Have the student tear out Student Page 205. He can decorate the sheet, and you should put it on the refrigerator or some other visible spot, to remind you and the student to review.

Coloring Page
. . . .
God Gives Us Good Things

Your parents care about you and give you good things. You can trust God to take care of you too, because God loves you even more than your parents do.

```
B S V D R T S L N A P W S Y C
R N O D U K E E P X R P N O R
E D C N S O E Y R O W H A N F
A M C A E B K N O C K R K J L
D G F B A P Z D P H Z E E E M
C H I L D R E N H F G H M N S
L R N F Q A O P E N V T Q O T
S F D K T I L T K L A W T P
G I V E N S G T S U I F I S H
```

Lesson 20 Go Fish Cards

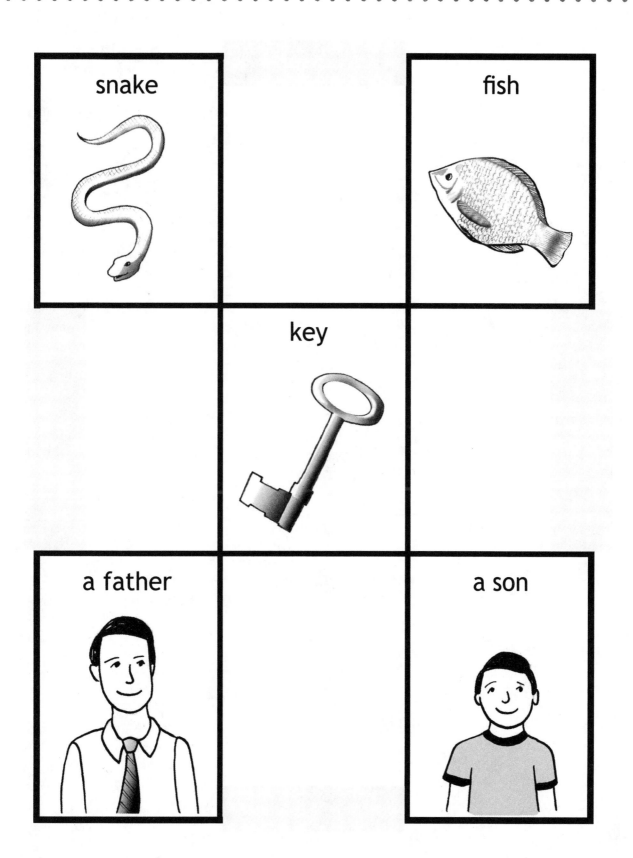

snake

fish

key

a father

a son

Lesson 20 Go Fish Cards

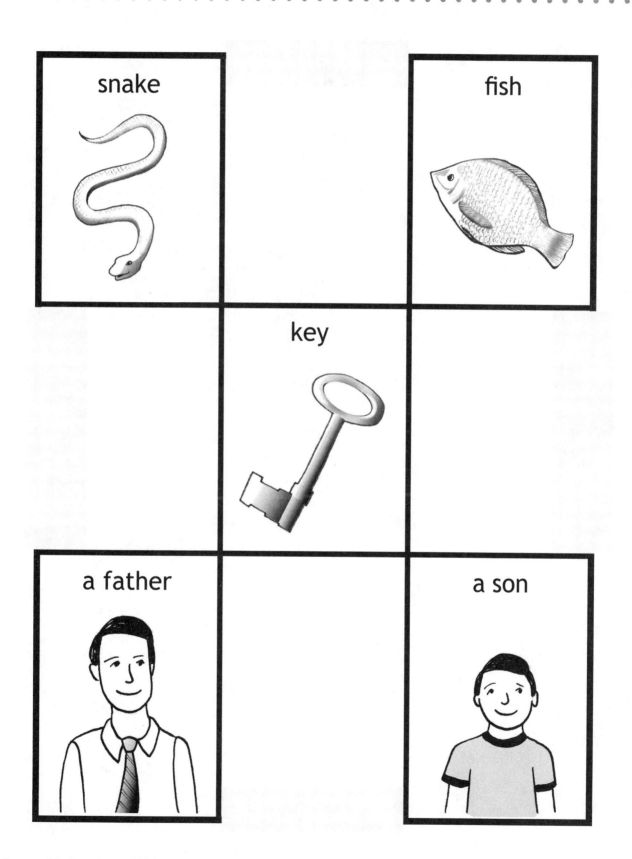

snake

fish

key

a father

a son

Lesson 20 Go Fish Cards

Lesson 20 Go Fish Cards

gift

bread

Bible

stone

door

Golden Rule

. . . .

Do to others whatever you would like them to do to you.

New Testament Books, Part IV

Matthew

Mark

Luke

John

Acts

Romans

First and Second Corinthians

Galatians

Ephesians

Philippians

Colossians

First and Second Thessalonians

First and Second Timothy

Titus

Philemon

Hebrews

James

First and Second Peter

First, Second, and Third John

Jude

Revelation

Matthew 7:7-12

Unit 5

Jesus' Early Life

Lesson 21: Jesus' Birth

Activities

Game Activity: **Birth of Jesus Scavenger Hunt**
Art History Project: **Picture Study of Tanner's** *The Annunciation*
Music Activity: **"O Come, O Come, Emmanuel"**
Memory Work: **Review the Books of the New Testament**
Coloring Page: **Mary and Joseph Are Married**

Game Activity

. . . .

Birth of Jesus Scavenger Hunt

Do this scavenger hunt around the house to retell the birth of Jesus.

Materials
- Birth of Jesus Scavenger Hunt Clues (Student Page 217)
- Scissors
- Pen or pencil
- Scotch tape

Directions

1   Have the student help you cut out the clues from Student Page 217. Then you will need to hide the clues from the student. Keep Clue 1 with you, and place the other clues as follows:
    Clue 2: inside the refrigerator
    Clue 3: on the student's pillow
    Clue 4: Inside the student's math book
    Clue 5: Near the student's toothbrush
    Clue 6: On the piano or other instrument, or on the stereo
    Clue 7: In the silverware drawer, on a spoon
    Note: The clues refer to common items and places in any house, but feel free to change any of the clues to fit your home's particularities.
2   Give the student the first clue. The student should follow each clue to find the next one, and should read aloud each clue when she finds it. As she follows the clues, she'll hear the story of the birth of Jesus.

3 For an added challenge when the student is finished, cut off the clue numbers at the top of each slip. Mix up the slips. See if the student can put the story back together in order.

Art History Project

• •

Picture Study of Tanner's *The Annunciation*

There are several paintings of the Annunciation (the angel announcing to Mary that she would be the mother of God's son) done by famous artists. This activity focuses on a painting by Henry Ossawa Tanner. Search the Web, if you like, to see others by Botticelli, Fra Angelico, Caravaggio, Titian, and Leonardo da Vinci. Tanner lived hundreds of years after most of the artists we will talk about in this book, but he is notable for his large body of religious work and the fact that he was the first African-American artist to win international acclaim.

Materials

- *The Annunciation* by Henry Ossawa Tanner (Student Page 219)

Directions

Show the student the painting on Student Page 219 as you tell about the artist and the painting and as you ask the following questions. You should definitely look at the color version too, if possible, at the Philadelphia Museum of Art website. Go to www.philamuseum.org/collections/search.html and search for "Tanner Annunciation." Encourage the student to answer the questions in complete sentences.

1 This painting is by Henry Ossawa Tanner, an American artist. It shows what Mr. Tanner thought it looked like when the angel appeared to Mary, to tell her that she was going to have a very special son, Jesus.
2 Can you point to Mary in this picture? To the angel?
3 What time of day do you think it is? (It is nighttime.)
4 Why do you think it is nighttime? (Mary is sitting on a bed, and it is dark in the room.)
5 What do you think Mary was doing just before the angel arrived? (She was sleeping.)
6 What does the angel look like? (The angel is brightly shining like a light or a fire.)
7 Look at the expression on Mary's face. Does she look scared?
8 Would you be scared if an angel came to talk to you?

Music Activity

• •

"O Come, O Come, Emmanuel"

Teach the students the song and the prophecies of Jesus it references.

Materials (for each student)

- "O Come, O Come, Emmanuel" lyrics coloring sheets (Student Pages 221 and 222)
- Coloring supplies

OPTIONAL: Recording of "O Come, O Come, Emmanuel." (A good recording can be found on the Robert Shaw Chamber Singers album *Songs of Angels: Christmas Hymns and Carols*, though it does not include all the verses listed below. Most modern recordings cut out at least two of these verses. YouTube also contains recordings of many choral and solo versions.)

Directions (spoken to the student)

1   Today we are going to learn about a very old Christmas carol. The tune is composed of several simple old melodies strung together. *(Note to Instructor: These are called antiphons, and they are the sung response, usually in Gregorian chant, to a psalm or a part of the church service.)* The song was originally sung in the Latin language. It had the name "Veni Emmanuel." We know it today as "O Come, O Come, Emmanuel." Remember from the lesson that "Emmanuel" means "God with us." That's what happened when Jesus came; God came to be with us! This song tells of all the prophecies, from many years before Jesus, that looked forward to the time when he would come.

2   Color the picture by the first verse of the song. This verse reminds us of the prophecy in Isaiah 7:14, "Behold, a virgin shall conceive, and bear a son, and shall call his name Emmanuel." The people of Israel had waited a long time for their Messiah to come and save them. *(Sing or play the recording of the first verse. It's OK if there is no musical accompaniment. The original hymn was meant to be sung that way!)*

O come, O come, Emmanuel
And ransom captive Israel
That mourns in lonely exile here
Until the Son of God appear
Rejoice! Rejoice! Emmanuel
Shall come to thee, O Israel.

3   Color in the picture next to the second verse. Jesus showed us God's wisdom, the right way to live. Proverbs 2:6 says, "For the Lord gives wisdom; from his mouth come knowledge and understanding." *(Play or sing this verse.)*

O come Thou wisdom from on high,
Who orders all things mightily;
To us the path of knowledge show,
And teach us in her ways to go.
Rejoice! Rejoice! Emmanuel
Shall come to thee, O Israel.

4   Color in the picture next to the third verse. This verse talks about "the Rod of Jesse," which comes from Isaiah 11:1. "There shall come forth a Rod from the stem of Jesse, and a Branch shall grow out of his roots." What do the words "stem," "branch," and "roots" have in common? They are all part of a tree. Have you ever heard of a family tree? It's a drawing that shows the names of children and their parents, their grandparents, their great-grandparents, and so on. You can see how people are related to each other across the generations. This is what the verse in Isaiah is talking about. Jesse was King David's

father. The prophecy tells us that a descendant of Jesse, someone down his family tree, will be the one to save his people. *(Play or sing this verse.)*

O come, Thou Rod of Jesse, free
Thine own from Satan's tyranny
From depths of Hell Thy people save
And give them victory o'er the grave
Rejoice! Rejoice! Emmanuel
Shall come to thee, O Israel.

5 Color in the picture next to the fourth verse. This verse talks about the prophecy that Zechariah made in Luke 1:78. Zechariah was John the Baptist's father. When John was a baby, his father prophesied that his son would prepare the way for the Messiah here on earth. Zechariah says, "The Dayspring from on high has visited us, to give light to those who sit in darkness." "Dayspring" means the first light of the morning, when the night is about to end. The Bible says that Jesus is like that. He is the light of the world. "Advent" means "arrival." *(Play or sing this verse.)*

O come, Thou Dayspring, come and cheer
Our spirits by Thine advent here
Disperse the gloomy clouds of night
And death's dark shadows put to flight.
Rejoice! Rejoice! Emmanuel
Shall come to thee, O Israel.

6 Color in the picture next to the fifth verse. This verse talks about the "Key of David," which comes from the prophecy in Isaiah 22:22. "The key of the house of David I will lay on his shoulder. So he shall open, and no one shall shut; and he shall shut, and no one shall open." Jesus is like a key because he opens up the way for us to live with God. *(Play or sing this verse.)*

O come, Thou Key of David, come,
And open wide our heavenly home;
Make safe the way that leads on high,
And close the path to misery.
Rejoice! Rejoice! Emmanuel
Shall come to thee, O Israel.

7 Color in the picture next to the sixth verse. This verse speaks about the time when God gave the Israelites his Law on Mount Sinai. The Israelites had been wandering the desert after the Lord had rescued them from the Egyptians. Moses went up the mountain; God spoke to him. Moses then brought God's Law to the people. (You can read Exodus 19 and 20 to set the scene; the laws themselves go up to chapter 32, but the Ten Commandments in Exodus 20:1–20 are the most important part.) *(Play or sing this verse.)*

O come, O come, Thou Lord of might,
Who to Thy tribes, on Sinai's height,
In ancient times did'st give the Law,

In cloud, and majesty and awe.
Rejoice! Rejoice! Emmanuel
Shall come to thee, O Israel.

8   Color in the picture next to the seventh verse. In this verse, Jesus is referred to as the "Desire of Nations." This comes from Haggai 2:7, "'I will shake all nations, and the desired of all the nations will come, and I will fill this house with glory,' says the Lord almighty." This verse also talks about Jesus bringing peace to the world. Isaiah 9:6 says, "For to us a child is born, to us a son is given . . . and He shall be called Wonderful Counselor, Mighty God, Everlasting Father, Prince of Peace." Jesus will end the fighting and quarreling between people and between countries. *(Play or sing this verse.)*

O come, Desire of Nations, bind
In one the hearts of all mankind;
Bid envy, strife, and quarrels cease
Fill all the world with heaven's peace.
Rejoice! Rejoice! Emmanuel
Shall come to thee, O Israel.

9   Sing the whole song with the student, or at least enough that she learns the tune and the refrain "Rejoice! Rejoice! Emmanuel shall come to thee, O Israel."

Memory Work

• •

Review the Books of the New Testament

Directions

Say to the student: "You have learned all of the books of the New Testament! Let's review them all to make sure they stay in your memory. The first five were Matthew, Mark, Luke, John, and Acts. Let's say those together."

[Together]: Matthew, Mark, Luke, John, Acts.

"Then we learned nine more books, the letters that Paul wrote to different groups of people. They were Romans, First and Second Corinthians, Galatians, Ephesians, Philippians, Colossians, First and Second Thessalonians. Let's say those together."

[Together]: Romans, First and Second Corinthians, Galatians, Ephesians, Philippians, Colossians, First and Second Thessalonians.

"Then we learned four more books, the letters Paul sent to specific people. Let's say those together."

[Together]: First and Second Timothy, Titus, Philemon.

"The last set of books was written to different churches and people as messages by God, by different writers. They were Hebrews, James, First and Second Peter, First, Second, and Third John, Jude, Revelation. Let's say those names together three times."

[Together, three times]: Hebrews, James, First and Second Peter, First, Second, and Third John, Jude, Revelation.

Coloring Page

• •

Mary and Joseph Are Married

An angel told Joseph not to be afraid to get married to Mary. She was going to have a special child, because of a miracle from God. So Joseph became her husband and helped raise this child, Jesus.

Birth of Jesus Scavenger Hunt

Clue 1:
Mary and Joseph promise to marry one another.
Go to the place where your drinks are kept cold.

Clue 2:
Before Mary and Joseph are married, Mary finds out she will have a baby.
Go to the place where you rest your head at night.

Clue 3:
When Joseph hears the news about Mary, he decides to divorce her quietly.
Open your math book.

Clue 4:
An angel appears to Joseph in a dream and tells him not to be afraid to marry Mary. Her baby will be the son of God.
Go to the place where you brush your teeth.

Clue 5:
The angel tells Joseph that the baby's name will be Jesus, and he will save his people from their sins.
Go to the place where you play music.

Clue 6:
All of this happens to fulfill the prophecy that a virgin would give birth to a son, who would be called Emmanuel, meaning "God with us."
Go to the place where you find something to help you eat yogurt, applesauce, or soup.

Clue 7:
When Joseph wakes up from his dream about the angel, he does everything the angel told him. He marries Mary, and when her son is born, they name him Jesus.
Congratulations! You are finished!

The Annunciation by Henry Ossawa Tanner

Philadelphia Museum of Art/Art Resource, NY

"O Come, O Come, Emmanuel"

VERSE 1
O come, O come, Emmanuel
And ransom captive Israel
That mourns in lonely exile here
Until the Son of God appear
Rejoice! Rejoice! Emmanuel
Shall come to thee, O Israel.

VERSE 2
O come Thou wisdom from on high,
Who orderest all things mightily;
To us the path of knowledge show,
And teach us in her ways to go.
Rejoice! Rejoice! Emmanuel
Shall come to thee, O Israel.

VERSE 3
O come, Thou Rod of Jesse, free
Thine own from Satan's tyranny
From depths of Hell Thy people save
And give them victory o'er the grave
Rejoice! Rejoice! Emmanuel
Shall come to thee, O Israel.

VERSE 4
O come, Thou Dayspring, come and cheer
Our spirits by Thine advent here
Disperse the gloomy clouds of night
And death's dark shadows put to flight.
Rejoice! Rejoice! Emmanuel
Shall come to thee, O Israel.

VERSE 5
O come, Thou Key of David, come,
And open wide our heavenly home;
Make safe the way that leads on high,
And close the path to misery.
Rejoice! Rejoice! Emmanuel
Shall come to thee, O Israel.

VERSE 6

O come, O come, Thou Lord of might,
Who to Thy tribes, on Sinai's height,
In ancient times did'st give the Law,
In cloud, and majesty and awe.
Rejoice! Rejoice! Emmanuel
Shall come to thee, O Israel.

VERSE 7

O come Desire of Nations, bind
In one the hearts of all mankind;
Bid envy, strife, and quarrels cease
Fill all the world with heaven's peace.
Rejoice! Rejoice! Emmanuel
Shall come to thee, O Israel.

Matthew 1:18–25

Lesson 22: God Protects Jesus from the King

Activities

Music and Craft Project: **The Gifts of the Wise Men**
Art History Project: **Botticelli's** *Adoration of the Magi*
Optional Craft Project: **Decorate a Gift Bag**
Game Activity: **Follow the Star**
Craft Project: **Make a Star**
Memory Work: **Review the Books of the New Testament**
Coloring Page: **The Magi Come to See Jesus**

Music and Craft Project

. . . .

The Gifts of the Wise Men

The gifts of the wise men foretold who Jesus would be and what would happen to him. Read the description of each gift and then listen to the verse from the American Christmas carol "We Three Kings of Orient Are," written by Rev. John Henry Hopkins in 1857. Then make a simple version of each gift.

Materials

- Audio recording of "We Three Kings of Orient Are"
- 5 oz. tub of play dough, any color (or make salt dough from the recipe in the Lesson 7 activities)
- Gold glitter
- Wax paper
- Baby powder
- Scented lotion

Directions

1   Play the song "We Three Kings of Orient Are." Remind the student that we don't know exactly how many magi there were, but many people think there were three because they brought three presents to Jesus. Lyrics can be found at www.carols.org.uk/we_three_kings_of_orient_are.htm. Encourage the student to sing along with the chorus.

2   Read the following description and verse to the student as he sculpts a small bowl out of the play dough (the size of an Oreo cookie). Then he should roll out a few small balls (the size of M&Ms). Sprinkle some gold glitter on a sheet of wax paper and roll the balls in the glitter until they are coated. Place the "gold" in the play-dough bowl.

Gold: A Gift for a King
Gold has always been precious and valuable. Because of this, gold was a gift fit for a king. Jesus is the King of Kings. "Jesus Christ, who is . . . the ruler of the kings of the earth." (Revelation 1:5)

Born a king on Bethlehem's plain
Gold I bring to crown him again
King forever, ceasing never
Over us all to reign

3   Read the following description and verse to the student as he sculpts another small bowl. Then he should sprinkle the baby powder into the bowl (this is the "frankincense").

Frankincense: A Gift for a Priest
Frankincense comes from the sap of a tree called the Boswellia tree, which grows in Africa and Arabia. Long ago, people found that when they took sap from this tree, dried it, and ground it into powder, the powder could be burned to make a smoke that smelled sweet. Incense was often burned in the temple, because people believed the smoke would carry their prayers to heaven. "The smoke from the incense, together with the prayers of the saints, went up before God from the angel's hand." (Revelation 8:4) The gift of frankincense foretells that Jesus will be the high priest who prays to God for us.

Frankincense to offer have I
Incense owns a deity nigh
Prayer and praising, all men raising
Worship him God on high

4   Read the following description and verse to the student as he sculpts another small bowl. Fill this bowl with a dab of scented lotion (this is the "myrrh").

Myrrh: A Gift for a Savior
The word "myrrh" is Arabic for "bitter." Myrrh comes from the resin of a tree found in North Africa. The Egyptians used myrrh to make perfumes, incense, and ointments. Myrrh ointment was used to preserve dead bodies. The gift of myrrh foretells that Jesus would one day die and be buried. He came back from the dead, though, as you will learn!

Myrrh is mine, its bitter perfume
Breathes a life of gathering gloom
Sorrowing, sighing, bleeding, dying
Sealed in a stone-cold tomb.

Art History Project

Botticelli's *Adoration of the Magi*

The scene of the worshipping wise men was a popular subject in Italian Renaissance art. Study the painting of one of the Florentine masters: Sandro Botticelli.

Materials

- Botticelli's *Adoration of the Magi* (see Student Page 233 or find a color version online at www.wga.hu/frames-e.html?/html/b/botticel/21/20adorat.html).

Directions

Show the student the painting on Student Page 233, or the color version you found on the Internet as you say the following. Encourage him to answer the questions in complete sentences.

1 Sandro Botticelli was born in Italy more than five hundred years ago. Look at the copy of *Adoration of the Magi*. The word "magi" is Greek for "scholars of magic" or "wise men." "Adoration" means "worshiping." These wise men came to worship the baby Jesus, because they knew he was not just any ordinary baby. He had been sent by God. The painting was done for a church in Botticelli's city and was paid for by some rich people in the town. As a way of saying "Thank you," Botticelli painted the picture so that some of the people in the scene looked like the important people in his city.

2 Find the baby Jesus. Where is he sitting? (In Mary's lap.)

3 His mother is looking down at him. Botticelli painted the picture in such a way that your attention would be drawn to Mary and Jesus.

4 Find Mary's husband Joseph. How is Joseph standing? (He is resting his head in his hand.)

5 Do you see the streams of light shining over Jesus? Point to them.

6 Where is that light coming from? *[If necessary, give this hint: It comes from the thing that guided the wise men to this spot.]* (The star.)

7 Do you see the wise man in a black robe kneeling directly in front of Jesus? He is not dressed like a wise man from that time! He is dressed in clothes from the time of Botticelli. This is Cosimo de'Medici. His sons are also in the painting. One kneels in the center of the painting with the big red cape draped over his back. The other kneeling wise man, facing him as if they are in conversation, may be a Medici son too. Lorenzo the Magnificent, the ruler of Botticelli's city at the time the painting was created, is in the picture too. You can only see the side of his face. He wears a black mantle with a red stripe.

8 The man who paid for the painting, Gaspare del Lama, also made it into the picture. He is hard to spot. Look at the right side of the painting, at the top row of men. Can you find the man with white hair who is looking right at you? His cloak is blue and you can see his hand. Can you tell what he is doing with his hand? (He is pointing at you.)

9 There is a man standing at the far right edge who is also looking at you. You can see his whole body—he has blonde hair and a yellow robe. This man is Botticelli, the artist who made this picture! Botticelli painted himself right into this painting.

Lesson 22: God Protects Jesus from the King   227

Optional Craft Project

. . . .

Decorate a Gift Bag

Materials

- Your copy of Botticelli's *Adoration of the Magi* (see Student Page 233)
- Scissors
- Coloring supplies
- Glue stick
- A gift bag large enough for the Botticelli picture to fit on the bag's front

Directions

1 Tear out Student Page 233 (or cut out the color copy you printed from the Internet).
2 Have the student color in the black-and-white picture with coloring supplies.
3 Have the student use the glue stick to attach the painting to the front of a gift bag.
4 Next time you or the student have a gift to give, place it in this bag!

Game Activity

. . . .

Follow the Star

This is a game about the wise men and King Herod trying to find the baby Jesus. The first half of it is a variation on "Follow the Leader," and the second half is like a competitive scavenger hunt.

Materials

- A star cut out of paper
- Crown (toy crown, or make your own using the template from Lesson 27)
- Baby doll

Directions

1 Hide the crown somewhere and don't tell the students where it is. (The crown stands for King Herod who lived in Jerusalem. The wise men went to him first.)
2 Hide the baby doll (the baby Jesus) somewhere in the house or outside while everyone closes their eyes.
3 Choose someone to be the Star (this person will be the leader for the first part of the game). Without letting anyone else hear, whisper to the Star-person the location of the crown. The Star has the paper star taped to his or her shirt and leads a line of students (the wise men) around the room/house/outside. If the Star steps over something, everyone else in line must too. If the Star crawls instead of walking for a while, or walks in a silly way, everyone else must too.

4 The Star should lead everyone to the place where the crown is (using a roundabout path to give time for lots of chances to "do what the Star does").

5 When the crown has been reached, give one student the crown. This student is King Herod.

6 Split the students into two teams. Make sure King Herod and the Star are on different teams. Everyone on the Star's team (except the Star) is a wise man, everyone on King Herod's team (except King Herod) is one of King Herod's soldiers.

7 Now King Herod and the Star must stand in one place. They can't move. Have the other students search for the baby doll. If a person sees the doll, he should not pick it up, but should run quickly back to his team captain (Herod or the Star) and touch that captain. Thus he scores a point.

8 The doll can be re-hidden in a different place every time a point is scored. The first team to five points wins. The wise men have to go look where the Star tells them, and King Herod's men have to go look where he/she tells them. Students can take turns being King Herod or the Star.

Craft Project

Make a Star

Here are two sets of instructions for an aluminum foil star or a paper star. The paper star is a little bit simpler to make.

Materials

- Aluminum foil
- Scissors
- Glue

Directions

1 Measure and cut eight 3½-inch squares (or eight 7-inch squares if you want something larger to work with) from paper or aluminum foil.

2 Fold each square in half. The folded edge should be at the top.

3 On each of the folded squares, fold the top left corner down in front. This should make a pocket that is triangle-shaped.

4 Fold the bottom right-hand corners up on each shape. You should now have 8 parallelograms. Hold one parallelogram upright with an open pocket at the top. Slide another parallelogram's triangular corner into that pocket at an angle to the right. Add a drop of glue to secure the two parallelograms together.

5 Continue to add parallelograms in the same way, working clockwise until the circle is complete. Allow glue to dry.

Alternate Version Five-point Star in One Snip

You can use foil or paper for this craft.

1   Help the student fold an 8½" x 10" piece of paper in half, so that the fold line is 8½" long. (NOTE: Make sure you are NOT using an 8½" x 11" piece of paper. If 8½" x 11" is all you have, cut an inch off of the bottom of the sheet of paper.)

2   Then, fold in half AGAIN and unfold, both vertically and horizontally. When the student has done this, the paper should still have its initial fold, from step 1, at the top, plus crease lines down the center, both vertically and horizontally.

3   Grab the top left corner and fold it down to touch the horizontal center line somewhere in the right half of the paper. Your fold should begin at the vertical center line at the top of the fold from step 1. Press down this fold.

4   Take hold of that same corner, and fold it in half back towards the left now, until it meets the left-hand edge. Press down this fold.

5   Take the right-hand side of your original rectangle, and fold it tightly over the left-hand triangles so that the fold is along the right edge of the left-side triangle.

6   Take the new far-left-hand corner, and fold it towards the right, until it meets the right-hand edge. Press down this fold.

7   Cut on the angle illustrated in the picture. Unfold the small piece of paper, and you will find your five-pointed star. (Try again if you haven't gotten it right.)

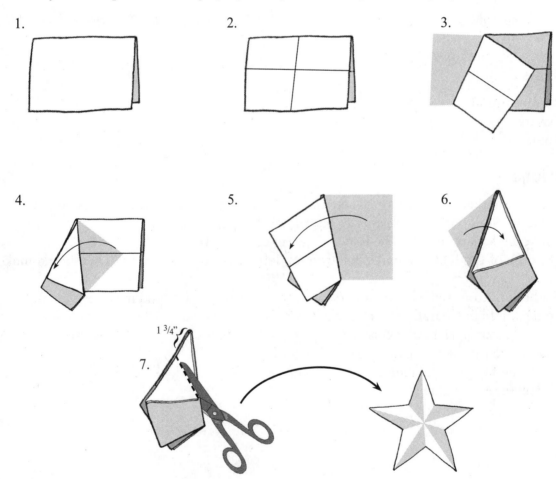

Memory Work

• •

Review the Books of the New Testament

Directions

Say to the student: "You have learned all of the books of the New Testament! Let's review them all to make sure they stay in your memory. The first five were Matthew, Mark, Luke, John, and Acts. Let's say those together."

[Together]: Matthew, Mark, Luke, John, Acts.

"Then we learned nine more books, the letters that Paul wrote to different groups of people. They were Romans, First and Second Corinthians, Galatians, Ephesians, Philippians, Colossians, First and Second Thessalonians. Let's say those together."

[Together]: Romans, First and Second Corinthians, Galatians, Ephesians, Philippians, Colossians, First and Second Thessalonians.

"Then we learned four more books, the letters Paul sent to specific people. Let's say those together."

[Together]: First and Second Timothy, Titus, Philemon.

"The last set of books was written to different churches and people as messages by God, by different writers. They were Hebrews, James, First and Second Peter, First, Second, and Third John, Jude, Revelation. Let's say those names together three times."

[Together, three times]: Hebrews, James, First and Second Peter, First, Second, and Third John, Jude, Revelation.

Coloring Page

• •

The Magi Come to See Jesus

These men studied the stars and planets to figure out what was going to happen in the world. God used a special star in the sky to tell them that Jesus was born. The magi traveled very far to see the baby.

Adoration of the Magi by Sandro Botticelli

Uffizi Gallery, Florence/Art Resource, NY

Matthew 2:1–12

Lesson 23: Jesus' Life Is in Danger

Activities

Game Activity: **Fleeing into Egypt**
Art Project: **"Escape to Egypt" Comic Strip**
Memory Work: **Review the Books of the New Testament**
Coloring Page: **Jesus' Family Flees to Egypt**

Game Activity

· ·

Fleeing into Egypt

Although the Bible does not give a detailed account of the holy family's journey to Egypt, many stories have been told about the path they took. Play this game to recount the events of the passage and encounter possible stops in Egypt along their trip. This game needs at least two players.

Materials

- Fleeing into Egypt Game Board (Student Pages 241 and 243)
- 1 dotted die
- A game piece for each player (like an M&M or a button)

Directions

1 Tear out Student Pages 241 and 243.
2 Roll the die to see which player goes first. The player with the highest roll becomes Player 1, and the player to her left is Player 2. Play continues clockwise.
3 Player 1 rolls the die and moves the designated number of spaces. If the player lands on a space with instructions, she must follow those.
4 The first player to get to the finish wins.

Art Project

· ·

"Escape to Egypt" Comic Strip

Have the students color the panels that tell the story of the Israelites' escape to Egypt (to flee a famine) and the holy family's parallel escape.

Materials (for each student)

- "Escape to Egypt" comic strip (Student Page 245)
- Coloring supplies
- Scissors
- Scotch tape
- OPTIONAL: Hole punch and 2 pieces of yarn, each 2 inches in length

Directions

1   Have the student color the "Escape to Egypt" comic strips (Student Page 245).
2   Help the student cut out both comic strips.
3   Use the Scotch tape to tape the right edge of the first strip (with one man whipping another man) to the left edge of the second strip (with a man with a staff leading a crowd of people). For best stability, use a piece of tape on the front/picture side of the paper and another piece on the back/blank side.
4   Go to the panel that says "Escape to Egypt" (on the far left). Keep this panel in front of you, and fold the rest of the strip behind it.
5   Continue to fold back the panels accordion-style until you can only see the "Escape to Egypt" panel in front of you. The student can now read both sides like a book.
6   Here are the captions that explain each panel:
"Escape to Egypt" (Title)
All the crops die. There is no food in Israel.
The Israelites go to Egypt where there is food.
The Israelites become slaves in Egypt.
God uses Moses to free the Israelites and lead them home.
King Herod wants to kill the baby Jesus.
Jesus' family escapes to Egypt where Herod can't find them.
After Herod dies, God calls the family back home.
7   OPTIONAL: Punch a hole through the top left corner of the booklet and the bottom left corner. Thread the yarn through all the layers and tie it in a bow. This will create a booklet effect.

Memory Work
· ·
Review the Books of the New Testament

Directions

Say to the student: "You have learned all of the books of the New Testament! Let's review them all to make sure they stay in your memory. The first five were Matthew, Mark, Luke, John, and Acts. Let's say those together."

[Together]: Matthew, Mark, Luke, John, Acts.

"Then we learned nine more books, the letters that Paul wrote to different groups of people. They were Romans, First and Second Corinthians, Galatians, Ephesians, Philippians, Colossians, First and Second Thessalonians. Let's say those together."

[Together]: Romans, First and Second Corinthians, Galatians, Ephesians, Philippians, Colossians, First and Second Thessalonians.

"Then we learned four more books, the letters Paul sent to specific people. Let's say those together."

[Together]: First and Second Timothy, Titus, Philemon.

"The last set of books was written to different churches and people as messages by God, by different writers. They were Hebrews, James, First and Second Peter, First, Second, and Third John, Jude, Revelation. Let's say those names together three times."

[Together, three times]: Hebrews, James, First and Second Peter, First, Second, and Third John, Jude, Revelation.

Coloring Page
• •
Jesus' Family Flees to Egypt

King Herod wanted to kill Jesus, so God warned Joseph to take Jesus and his mother and run away to the country of Egypt.

Fleeing into Egypt

Fleeing into Egypt

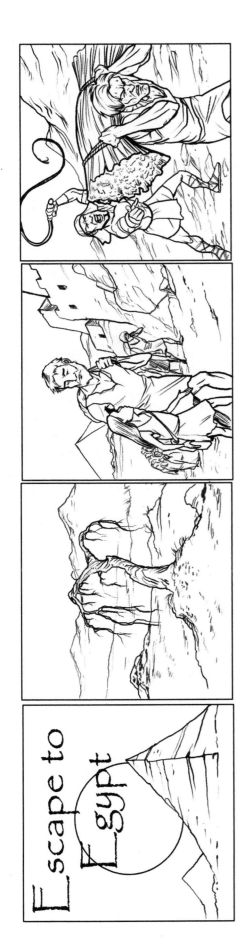

Matthew 2:13–15

Lesson 24: Jesus and His Family Come Back Home

Activities

Game Activity: **Crack the Code**
History Project: **Make Coins from the Time of Herod the Great**
Game Activity: **"Return to Israel" Maze**
Memory Work: **Review the Books of the New Testament**
Coloring Page: **Jesus Grows Up in a Small Town**

Game Activity

· ·

Crack the Code

Crack the code to reveal the secret message.

Materials

- Secret message (Student Page 253)
- Pencil

Directions

1   Tell the student to examine the secret message on Student Page 253. All the vowels have been replaced by numbers.
2   Help the student use the key to substitute the vowel for the corresponding number.
3   Answer key: *Jesus is like Moses. They both left home because they were in danger and came back when it was safe. They both delivered God's people.*

History Project

Make Coins from the Time of Herod the Great

No one knows what Herod the Great looked like. There is an etching of him in most history books, but this is a fictional portrait by an unnamed artist, made well after Herods' death (so it probably looks nothing like him). There are a number of coins from his time, though they do not have his face on them. The student will color the coins and cut them out to make his own ancient money.

Materials

- Coins from the Time of Herod the Great (Student Page 255)
- White cardstock or plain white index cards
- Scissors
- Glue
- Crayons

Directions

1. Tear out Student Page 255. Have the student look at the various coins from Herod's time. Notice that the front and back of each coin are shown. Help the student cut the coins out, but make sure you keep the front and back picture from each coin together after cutting (so they don't get mixed up).
2. Trace each coin onto an index card, and cut out. Now you will have three white circles, one for each coin. Keep the coin pictures and their corresponding white circles together.
3. The student should glue the front and back picture of the coin onto the front and back of the cardstock circle he has cut out, and then he can color the coins with the crayons. Pick bright colors and use at least three colors on each circle.

Game Activity

"Return to Israel" Maze

Materials

- Pencil
- "Return to Israel" Maze (Student Page 257)

Directions

Have the student use a pencil to help Joseph and his family return to Israel from Egypt.

Memory Work

Review the Books of the New Testament

Directions

Say to the student: "You have learned all of the books of the New Testament! Let's review them all to make sure they stay in your memory. The first five were Matthew, Mark, Luke, John, and Acts. Let's say those together."

[Together]: Matthew, Mark, Luke, John, Acts.

"Then we learned nine more books, the letters that Paul wrote to different groups of people. They were Romans, First and Second Corinthians, Galatians, Ephesians, Philippians, Colossians, First and Second Thessalonians. Let's say those together."

[Together]: Romans, First and Second Corinthians, Galatians, Ephesians, Philippians, Colossians, First and Second Thessalonians.

"Then we learned four more books, the letters Paul sent to specific people. Let's say those together."

[Together]: First and Second Timothy, Titus, Philemon.

"The last set of books was written to different churches and people as messages by God, by different writers. They were Hebrews, James, First and Second Peter, First, Second, and Third John, Jude, Revelation. Let's say those names together three times."

[Together, three times]: Hebrews, James, First and Second Peter, First, Second, and Third John, Jude, Revelation.

Coloring Page

Jesus Grows Up in a Small Town

When it was safe for Jesus' family to come back from Egypt, they moved to a little town called Nazareth. Jesus didn't grow up in a kingly palace; he grew up in this little town.

Secret Message

Use the key to substitute the numbers in the code for the letters A, E, I, O, and U. Write them in the blanks.

Key:

A=1 E=2 I=3 O=4 U=5

Message:

J ___ S ___ S   ___ S   L ___ K ___   M ___ S ___ S.

J2S5S   3S   L3K2   M4S2S.

TH ___ Y   B ___ TH   L ___ FT   H ___ M ___
B ___ C ___   ___ S ___   TH ___ Y   W ___ R ___
___ N   D ___ NG ___ R

TH2Y B4TH L2FT   H4M2 B2C15S2   TH2Y   W2R2   3N
D1NG2R

___ ND   C ___ M ___   B ___ CK   WH ___ N
___ T   W ___ S   S ___ F ___.

1ND   C1M2   B1CK WH2N   3T W1S S1F2.

TH ___ Y   B ___ TH   D ___ L ___ V ___ R ___ D
G ___ D'S   P ___ ___ PL ___.

TH2Y B4TH D2L3V2R2D   G4D'S P24PL2.

Coins of Herod the Great

"Return to Israel" Maze

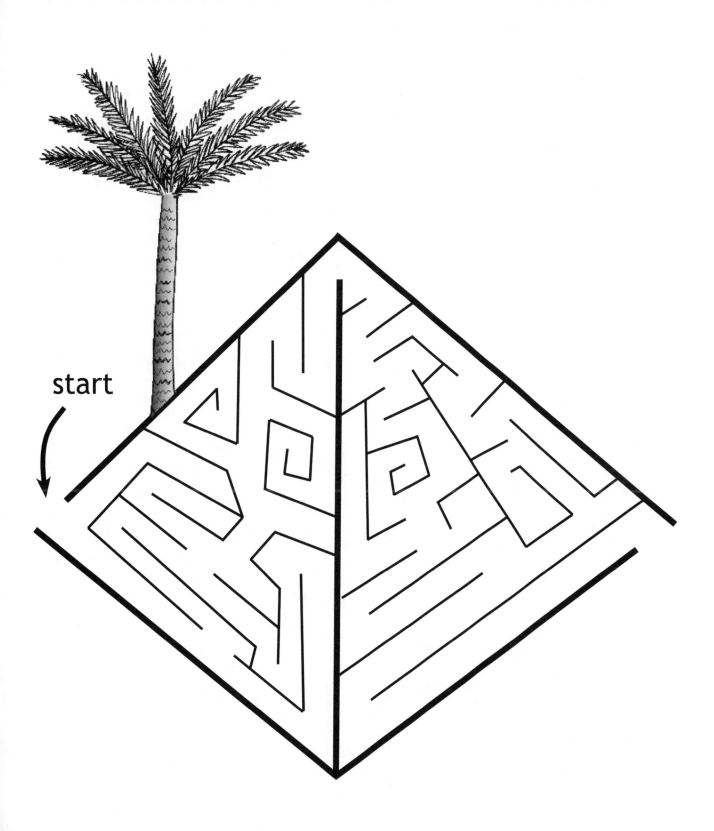

start

Matthew 2:19–23

Unit 6

Jesus' Disciples

Lesson 25: Jesus' First Disciples

Activities

Game Activity: **Go Fishing**
Art History Project: **Duccio's** *The Calling of the Apostles Peter and Andrew*
Art Project: **Paint with Egg Tempera**
Craft Project: **Make a Cloth Fish**
Game Activity: **Fishers of Men**
Coloring Page: **Jesus Calls Two Fishermen to Be His Disciples**

Game Activity

• •

Go Fishing

This activity uses a magnetic fishing pole, even though the disciples used nets to catch their fish.

Materials

- Unsharpened pencil
- Scotch tape
- String (about 12 inches long)
- Small magnet (U-shaped magnets work well, but you can use any magnet you can tie a string to)
- 8 small metal paper clips
- Aluminum foil
- Fish pattern (Student Page 267)
- Pencil
- Big bowl (e.g., punch bowl, your largest mixing bowl)
- Water
- Scissors

Directions

1 Fill the bowl with water. Set aside.
2 Cut out the fish pattern on Student Page 267.
3 Tear off a square sheet of aluminum foil, at least 4" x 4". Fold it in half once, and then fold it in half again.
4 Help the student trace the fish pattern onto the folded aluminum foil and cut it out. She should have four fish.

5 Repeat steps 3 and 4 with another piece of aluminum foil. The student should now have eight fish.
6 Help the student fasten a paper clip to the "nose" of each fish. Drop the fish in the bowl of water.
7 Tie one end of the string to the end of the unsharpened pencil. Secure with tape.
8 Tie the other end of the string to the magnet. This is the student's "fishing pole."
9 Have the student try to catch all the fish in the bowl by attracting the paper clips with the magnet. Or to make it a competitive game for two players, make a second fishing pole and see who can catch the most fish in thirty seconds.

Art History Project
• •

Duccio's *The Calling of the Apostles Peter and Andrew*

Learn about Duccio's Maestà *altarpiece and the individual painting in it of Peter, Andrew, and Jesus. The project after this one involves making some egg tempera paint, Duccio's paint of choice.*

Materials

* *The Calling of the Apostles Peter and Andrew* (Student Page 269)
* Bible

Directions

Show the student the painting on Student Page 269 as you say the following. Encourage the student to answer the questions in complete sentences.

1 Duccio di Buoninsegna was an artist born in Siena, Italy, around 1255. Not much is known about his life; he left no journals or letters behind, but his painting was very influential. Although the city of Siena was known for the skill of its painters, Duccio is considered the finest of them all. Today, only a handful of his paintings remain. One of them, the *Maestà*, is considered his masterpiece. The *Maestà* is an altarpiece that was created for the cathedral of Siena. An altarpiece is in the front part of a church, where everybody can see it, so it needs to be very beautiful. The *Maestà* is enormous: 7 feet high and 14 feet long, painted on the front and the back. That means it is taller than your parents and longer than a van. The front shows Mary and the baby Jesus surrounded by the saints and angels. The back has 43 separate panels that tell of Mary's life and Jesus' life.
2 The altarpiece stayed where it was in Siena's cathedral until 1711, when it was sawn apart to divide it between 2 altars. Some of the paintings were damaged when this was done; others were sold or lost altogether.
3 One of the panels on the back of the *Maestà* was a scene from the life of Jesus: *The Calling of the Apostles Peter and Andrew*. The panel, painted with egg tempera on wood, is now in a museum in the United States.
4 Now try to answer these questions. If you need hints, I will read you some of the Bible story from this week's lesson.

5 Who is the man standing on the shore? (That is Jesus.) [If the student can't remember, read the first sentence of Matthew 4:18 aloud.]

6 Who are the two men in the boat? (They are Peter and Andrew.) [If the student can't remember, read the first sentence of Matthew 4:18 aloud.]

7 How were Peter and Andrew related to each other? (They were brothers.) [If the student can't remember, read the first sentence of Matthew 4:18 aloud.]

8 What was their job? (They were fishermen.) [If the student can't remember, read the second sentence of Matthew 4:18 aloud.]

9 What are they holding? (They are holding a net.)

10 Is the net full of fish or is it empty? (It is full of fish.)

11 Look at Jesus' hands. What does it look like he is doing with his raised hand? (He is calling them over to him; Gesturing "Come here.") [If the student can't remember, read Matthew 4:19 aloud.]

12 Look at Peter's hand. He has dropped the net from one hand and is raising it toward Jesus. What do you think he is doing? (Saying hello to Jesus; Reaching out to Jesus.)

Art Project

• •

Paint with Egg Tempera

For the best egg tempera, use powder tempera (you can buy this at art supply stores, at Amazon.com, or at Sargentart.com). You can also use ground chalk. The bright colors work best. Crush the chalk into a powder with a mortar and pestle (or use a round rock in an old bowl).

Materials

- Pigment (powder tempera or ground chalk, see above note), in at least three colors
- Plastic or Styrofoam egg container
- 3 or more eggs (1 egg for each color you create)
- Paintbrush
- Water
- Small whisk or fork
- Tablespoon
- Liquid measuring cup
- OPTIONAL: Egg separator

Directions

1 Have the student crack an egg. Separate the yolk (this is where an egg separator comes in handy). Dump the yolk into the measuring cup and add 1 Tbsp. water. Whisk until light and frothy.

2 Pour a small amount of pigment (powder tempera or chalk dust) into a well in the egg container. Add a few drops of water and mix it into a paste. Try to work out any lumps.

3 Let the student pour the egg yolk into the pigment-well and mix with a fork until smooth.

4 Repeat steps 1–3 to make the remaining colors. You can even make new colors by combining the pigment powders.

5 Say to the student, "Now you are ready to paint! Try painting your own panel of *The Calling of the Apostles Peter and Andrew*. Use a pencil to draw a man with a net fishing in the sea. Then use the egg tempera to paint your drawing. Don't try to put in too many little details, because the paint will cover them up."

Craft Project

• •

Make a Cloth Fish

Make a fabric fish filled with Swedish fish gummy candy. If you prefer something less sugary, Goldfish snack crackers are popular with this age group.

Materials (for each student)

- String or ribbon (about 8" long)
- 5½" x 8" foam sheet
- Scissors
- Fabric glue (school glue also works)
- 8" x 8" fabric square, any color or pattern
- Generous handful of Swedish fish (or Goldfish crackers)
- White paper and a black marker OR two wiggle eyes

Directions

1 Spread out the fabric on the table (if you use printed fabric, the plain side should face up).
2 Have the student place the candy/crackers in the center of the fabric.
3 Gather up the corners of the fabric to make a pouch that holds the candy/crackers inside.
4 Help the student tie a string or ribbon around the neck of the pouch so the candy fish/crackers are secure.
5 Now lay the bag on its side. The top/opening of the bag is now the "tail" of a fish, and the wide part where most of the candy/crackers are located is the body/head of a fish. But this fish still needs a face. So . . .
6 Cut out a mouth, two fins, and two eyes from the foam sheet.
7 Glue the mouth in the front and a fin on each side of the fish's "body." Glue a wiggle eye to either side of the "head," or if you prefer, make eyes using the white paper and black marker, and glue them on.
8 Let dry.

Game Activity

Fishers of Men

This game is best played outside.

Materials

- Two blankets
- Multiple action figures (or stuffed animals, or baby dolls, or anything heavy enough to toss that the students could pretend is a man)

Directions

1 Make two teams (they can be teams of just one, but more than one person per team works much better).
2 Give each team an unfolded blanket, and have the team members work together to hold it stretched out.
3 Say, "Ready . . . set . . . go!" and throw two of the action figures as high as possible into the air, one from each hand. The students' job is to catch the figures in the blanket. For every figure a team successfully catches in the blanket, give that team a point. The first one to lead by three points wins.
4 (Note: You can re-use the same action figures over and over, or you can use a bunch of different ones and make the students catch more while they already have some in their net, thus making the game more difficult.)

Coloring Page

Jesus Calls Two Fishermen to Be His Disciples

Simon (later called Simon Peter) and his brother Andrew were working as fishermen when Jesus told them to come learn from him instead.

Fish Pattern

The Calling of the Apostles Peter and Andrew by Duccio

Used by permission of the National Gallery of Art, Washington, DC

Matthew 4:18–22

Lesson 26: Jesus Is a Friend of the Shunned

Activities

Game Activity: **"Don't Judge on Appearances" Pick and Choose Game**
Prayer Activity: **Praying for Others**
Memory Work: **The Twelve Disciples, Part I**
Coloring Page: **Jesus Is a Friend to All Kinds of People**

Game Activity
. . . .
"Don't Judge on Appearances" Pick and Choose Game

Jesus didn't pick the most "impressive" people to be his disciples. No one but Jesus thought Matthew the tax collector would be a good choice, but Jesus didn't make his choice based on appearances. Play this game with the student to drive home the age-old lesson: don't judge a book by its cover!

Materials

- Appetizing snack for the student, set in a plain, old, beat-up box
- Unappetizing snack (beans, unpopped popcorn kernels, broken old crackers), wrapped in a gift box with pretty paper and a big bow
- 2 opaque tins or jars with lids; put 20 pennies in one jar and 1 quarter in another
- Baking chocolate
- Cracker

Directions

1   Tell the student, "Today, you are going to make some choices." Show the student the two boxes with the snacks inside (which he can't see, of course). Tell him there is a snack in each box. Ask (or, for a class, take a vote): Which snack would the student most like to eat? (Probably he'll choose the nicely wrapped box.) Set both aside to open in a minute.
2   Show the tins or jars with the coins inside. Tell the student to shake each jar (if the jars are identical, put a number 1 and 2 on each jar, respectively). After the student has shaken the jar, ask which jar has more money inside. Set these jars aside for the moment.
3   Give the student a cracker and a piece of baking chocolate. Tell him not to touch them. Ask the student to describe what he thinks the cracker will taste like (salty, crunchy).

Ask him to tell you what he thinks the chocolate will taste like (sweet, creamy). Tell him he may choose EITHER the cracker or the chocolate to eat. He must choose whichever one he thinks will be more delicious. (Most students will choose the chocolate.)

4   Let the student taste the baking chocolate and give his reaction (if he chose the cracker, encourage him to taste the chocolate as well and give his opinion). What does the baking chocolate taste like? What did he expect it to taste like? (Sweet!) Why did he think it would be sweet? (Because it looked like chocolate candy, which is sweet!) Tell him, "You can't judge something by the way it looks. You may have thought this chocolate would be sweet because of the way it looks, but it wasn't!"

5   Take out the jars of coins. Shake them for the student. Point out the one he thought had more money inside. (He most likely chose the jar with pennies.) Ask him why he thought that. (You can hear that there are a lot of coins inside.) Open each jar and have the student count the money inside. The result is that the jar with a single coin actually has more money in it than the jar with all the pennies. "You can't judge something based on appearances. The penny jar sounded like it had lots of money, but it actually had less than the other jar!"

6   Tell the student it is time for a snack. Take out the nicely wrapped box (the one the student probably chose). Have him unwrap the box. Once he sees what is inside, ask him, "Is this what you expected?" Then have him open the plain box with the real snack. Ask the student, "Which box did you think would have the better snack? Why?"

7   Bring the activity back to the Bible lesson. "You can't judge something or someone by appearances. Jesus didn't. He didn't choose the important or impressive-looking people to be his disciples. He chose fishermen and a tax collector whom everyone hated! But Jesus wasn't looking at the outside; he was looking into the heart of a person, and at what that person truly needed." (Now let the student eat the yummy snack.)

Prayer Activity

Praying for Others

Materials

- Construction paper or poster board
- Crayons, markers, or colored pencils

Directions

1   Using a large piece of construction paper or poster board, help the student make a list of people in his life who haven't found God or who (as far as you and the student know) don't have a relationship with God in their lives. This could be a simple list of people who, the child knows, don't share your faith, such as grandparents who don't attend church, neighbors who are atheists, etc.

2   At the bottom of your list write in large letters the following sentence, taken from this week's lesson, "The people who we think are the furthest away from God, are the ones Jesus came to rescue."

3   Have the student draw, color, or paste a decorative border around the list, and hang it up on a wall near his bed to remember to pray for these people each night this week. The

student could thank God for how much God loves these people (and for how much God loves him, too). He could ask God that the people would see how much Jesus loves them, and/or that God would help the student show kindness and love to them.

Memory Work
• •
The Twelve Disciples, Part I

Materials

- The Twelve Disciples, Part I (Student Page 277)

Directions

Say to the student: "In the last lesson, we heard about some of the people Jesus called to come with him. Many people listened to what Jesus had to say, but he invited a special group of twelve men, called the twelve disciples, to spend all their time traveling with him, listening and learning from him, and then telling people about him. (Disciple means learner or student.) These twelve disciples told people, who told people, who told people, and so on until someone told *you* about Jesus. This week we're going to learn the names of six of these disciples."

"Here are the first six names *(read these six names to the student twice)*: Simon Peter, Andrew, James, John, Philip, Thomas."

"Now let's repeat each of those names, so you'll know how to say them." *(Repeat each name with the student.)*

"Now let's say that list five times."

(Together, five times): Simon Peter, Andrew, James, John, Philip, Thomas.

Have the student tear out Student Page 277. He can decorate the sheet, and you should put it on the refrigerator or some other visible spot, to remind you and the student to review.

Coloring Page
• •
Jesus Is a Friend to All Kinds of People

In the story we read today, Jesus ate and talked with people to whom no one else was kind. Here he is eating a meal at Matthew's house.

The Twelve Disciples, Part I

Simon Peter

Andrew

James

John

Philip

Thomas

Matthew 9:9–13

Lesson 27: Philip and Nathanael

Activities

Map Activity/History Project: **Where Are You From?**
Craft Project: **Make a King's Crown**
Craft Project: **Nathanael Telescope**
Memory Work: **Review the Twelve Disciples, Part I**
Coloring Page: **Philip Brings Nathanael to Meet Jesus**

Map Activity/History Project
• •
Where Are You From?

Nathanael was skeptical of Jesus because Jesus came from the small, insignificant town of Nazareth. Do this project so the student can see where he is from, and also where his family is from. You will need to know where the child's parents and grandparents were born.

Materials

- Map of your state/province
- Globe or world map
- "Where Are You From?" (Student Page 285)
- Computer with Internet access

Directions

1 Tell the student, "Jesus was from the tiny town of Nazareth, and Nathanael at first thought no one special could come from there. Let's find out about where you and your family are from." Ask the student to tell you the city and state/province where she was born (if she doesn't know this already, now is a good time to learn). Find it on the state/province map. Fill in the name of the city and state/province on the "You" blank on Student Page 285.

2 Use the Internet to find out the following information about the town or city in which the student was born (you can use a search engine, go to your chamber of commerce or city website, or use a site such as <u>www.city-data.com</u> or <u>www.idcide.com</u>).

a. Closest major city (you could use a map for this).

b. Size of population (finding the exact number is good, but since such large numbers are often meaningless to young students, you could convert the numbers into such classifications as Really Really Huge, Very Small, etc.).

c. Something that this city is famous for.

3 Fill in the information on the "Where Are You From?" sheet.

4 Find out the same information about the cities where the student's parents and grandparents were born. Help the student fill them out on the "Where Are You From?" sheet.

Craft Project

• •

Make a King's Crown

Nathanael called Jesus "King of Israel." Jesus didn't wear a crown, but it is still a recognizable symbol of royalty. Make this king's crown to remind the student that Jesus is the king over all kings.

Materials

- Crown template (Student Page 287)
- Cardstock or thin cardboard (like a cereal box)
- Pencil
- Scissors
- Glue
- Construction paper (or take it up a step and use gold or silver wrapping paper)
- Stapler
- Any of the following: self-adhesive gems, beads, buttons, pasta shapes, glitter, or glitter glue

Directions

1 Have the student cut out the crown template on Student Page 287.

2 Trace this template onto the cardstock and cut out.

3 Trace the template onto the construction or wrapping paper and cut out.

4 Have the student glue the paper to the cardstock crown.

5 Let the student use the decorative items (gems, beads, buttons, etc.) and glue to "bejewel" the crown.

6 Cut out a strip of cardstock that is about 1–2" wide and at least 12" long. Cover with construction or wrapping paper, if you wish.

7 Staple one end of the cardstock strip to one end of the crown. Fit the crown around the student's head and staple the strip to the other side of the crown.

Craft Project

• •

Nathanael Telescope

Jesus knew Nathanael long before he met him face to face. Jesus told Nathanael he had seen him sitting under the fig tree. Make this "telescope" to look through and see what Jesus saw: Nathanael sitting under the tree.

Materials

- Empty paper-towel or toilet-paper tube
- Nathanael picture (Student Page 289)
- Tracing paper or parchment paper (about a 5" square or circle)
- Sharpened pencil
- Rubber band
- Black marker
- OPTIONAL: Paint OR wrapping paper, tape, and scissors

Directions

1 Lay the parchment or tracing paper over the Nathanael picture (Student Page 289). Help the student use the pencil to trace the picture onto the parchment.
2 If the student wishes to decorate the paper-towel tube, she can now paint it or cover it with wrapping paper.
3 With the black marker, help the student write "Jesus saw Nathanael" on one side of the tube and "Jesus sees me" on the other side.
4 Center the parchment on one end of the paper tube so the picture is visible through the opposite end of the tube. Let the student fasten the parchment to the tube with the rubber band.
5 Help the student point the paper-covered end of the tube at a light source and peer through the open end. Say, "You can now see Nathanael. Jesus saw Nathanael before he ever met him. And Jesus sees you, too!"

Memory Work

• •

Review the Twelve Disciples, Part I

Directions

Say to the student, "In the last lesson, you learned the names of six of the people who Jesus chose to learn from him and tell people about him. Let's review those names by saying them together, three times."

(Together, three times): Simon Peter, Andrew, James, John, Philip, Thomas.

Coloring Page

• •

Philip Brings Nathanael to Meet Jesus

Philip was so excited about Jesus that he brought his friend Nathanael to meet him. But even before Nathanael came, Jesus already knew who he was!

Where Are You From?

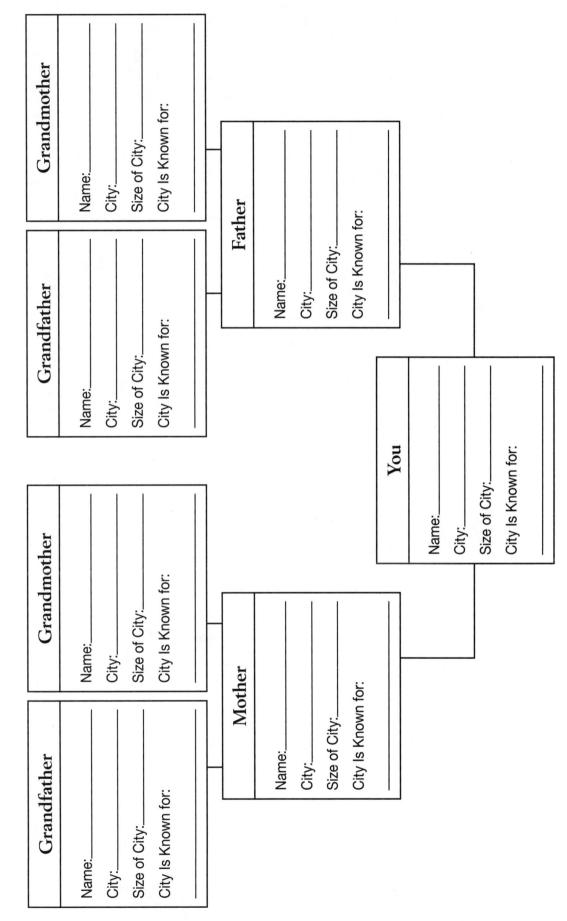

Crown

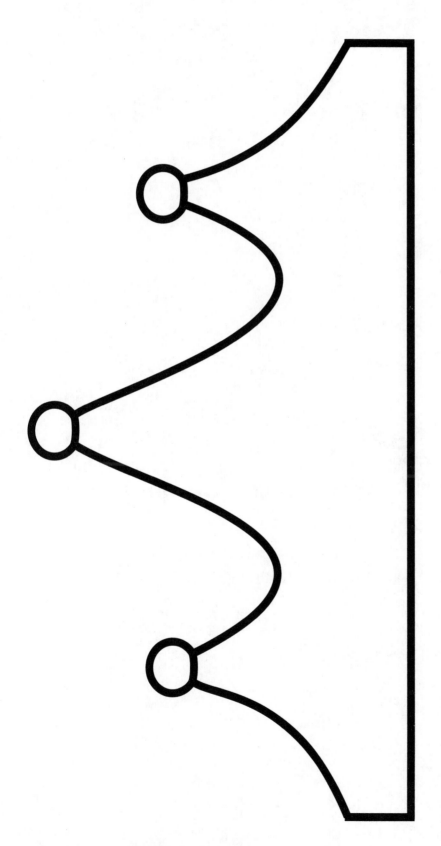

Nathanael Telescope

John 1:43–51

Lesson 28: A Story of Two Sisters

Activities

Service Activity: **"Serving God" Match-up**
Service Activity: **Show Hospitality**
Craft Project: **Make a Martha, Mary, and Jesus Mini Puppet Theater**
Cooking Project: **Make First-century Food for a Guest**
Memory Work: **Review the Twelve Disciples, Part I**
Coloring Page: **Jesus and the Two Sisters**

Service Activity

• •

"Serving God" Match-up

This lesson emphasized that there is more than one way to serve the Lord. This activity shows the student the many ways a person can serve God in his community.

Materials

- "Serving God" Match-Up (Student Page 297)
- Pencil

Directions

1 On the left side of the page is a column of people with different talents and gifts. The right column lists ways to serve God in the church and community.
2 Ask the student to draw a line from the left-hand column (gifts) to the right hand column (service), matching the gifts with the corresponding services. There could be multiple matches for a gift. The point is not to "get it right," but to start a discussion on the different ways people can serve God.

Answer Key: 1) b, 2) i, 3) c or e, 4) g or d, 5) d, 6) h or a, 7) e, 8) f, 9) a

Service Activity
. . . .
Show Hospitality

Martha was right to be hospitable, even though she became too focused on whether Mary was doing her fair share of the work. In this activity, the student (or, ideally, a group of students) will practice hospitality like a good first-century (or twenty-first-century) host, and will learn the value of all kinds of service (actively preparing a home and meal, and personally listening to a guest).

Materials

- Student Page 299
- Hospitality items: Something to drink, a snack, a cushion or pillow, a warm washcloth, dishes

Directions

1   Select one person (perhaps a neighbor, teacher, or friend from outside the class) to be the "guest."
2   Cut out the cards on Student Page 299. (Use the blank cards to add additional tasks if you would like to make some up.)
3   Distribute the cards to everyone who is not the guest. One player should receive the "Sit and talk with your guest" card, and the others should all receive the various serving cards. (If only one student and one instructor are playing, then that student can do as many of the steps as you think are appropriate while the instructor sits and eats the snack.)
4   Follow the instructions on the cards. Everyone will end up busily getting things for the guest, except for one who gets to sit, eat and drink, and talk to the guest.
5   After the guest has had a nice "visit," talk to the students about how both serving the guest and listening to what the guest had to say were important, even if the servers felt that they were doing all the work.

Craft Project
. . . .
Make a Martha, Mary, and Jesus Mini Puppet Theater

Reenact the story from the lesson with these easy-to-make puppets.

Materials (for each student)

- Jesus, Mary, and Martha cutouts (Student Page 301)
- Empty shoebox
- 2 craft sticks/Popsicle sticks
- Glue stick
- Scissors
- Coloring supplies (markers, colored pencils, or crayons)
- Small strip of cardstock (about 1" x 4")
- OPTIONAL: Wrapping paper, construction paper

Directions

1 Color the Jesus, Mary, and Martha figures on Student Page 301. Cut out.
2 Glue the Jesus figure to the top half of a craft stick. Do the same with Martha.
3 Bend the strip of cardstock in half. Glue the Mary figure to the top half of the cardstock. Set puppets aside.
4 Remove the lid from the shoebox. Turn the shoebox on its side so the open part faces you. This is the orientation of the puppet theater. Cut a slit in the "bottom" of the theater (the former side of the box). The slit should be centered horizontally and should run most of the way across (leave about 1" on either side). The slit needs to be wide enough for the puppets to fit through. Try fitting a stick puppet through; widen the slit if needed.
5 OPTIONAL: Decorate the inside of the theater by gluing wrapping paper or construction paper to it. You can add things to make it look more like a house: a kitchen area, a table, windows, additional people around where Jesus stands, etc.
6 Get the Mary figure. Bend back the bottom half of the cardstock and glue it to the bottom of the puppet theater, in FRONT of the slit and toward one end of the theater. (If you drew a kitchen, make sure Mary is on the opposite side of the room.)
7 Slide in the other puppet figures and retell the story from the lesson. The student can ask someone else to hold the theater or place the theater in his own lap to perform to himself.

The student should add dialogue, imagining what the characters might have said:

Martha invites Jesus inside.

Martha goes to work cooking a meal, grumbling to herself about Mary.

Jesus teaches while Mary listens.

Martha repeatedly asks Mary for help, but Mary refuses.

Martha asking Jesus, "Lord, don't you care that my sister has left me to do the work by myself? Tell her to help me!"

Jesus responding to Martha, "Martha, Martha, you are worried and upset about many things, but only one thing is needed. Mary has chosen what is better, and it will not be taken away from her."

(The important thing is that the student can replay the gist of the story, not that he gets the words exactly right.)

Cooking Project

. . . .

Make First-century Food for a Guest

Ingredients

- ½ pound of red lentils
- 5½ c. vegetable broth
- 1 c. finely chopped onion
- 1 c. olive oil
- 2 bay leaves
- 1 clove of minced garlic

- 1 tsp. kosher salt or sea salt
- Ground pepper to taste
- OPTIONAL: ½ tsp. ground cumin

Directions

1 In a pot, have the student combine the broth, bay leaves, onion, cumin, salt, pepper, and garlic.
2 Bring to a slow boil over medium heat and add the lentils and oil.
3 Reduce the heat and simmer partially covered for 1 to 1½ hours, or until lentils are done. Remove from the heat, take out the bay leaves, and serve.

Memory Work

Review the Twelve Disciples, Part I

Directions

Say to the student, "You have already learned the names of six of the people who Jesus chose to learn from him and tell people about him. Let's review those names by saying them together, three times."

(Together, three times): Simon Peter, Andrew, James, John, Philip, Thomas.

Coloring Page

Jesus and the Two Sisters

When Jesus was at Mary and Martha's house, Martha was upset that Mary was listening to Jesus instead of helping to make the meal. Jesus said that Martha shouldn't be upset. Both sisters were doing good things, but they were different things.

Serving God Match-Up

Draw a line from the person with a gift to the way that person could serve God.

PERSON AND GIFT

1. A good musician

2. A good cook

3. A friendly person

4. Someone good at math

5. A good teacher

6. Someone who enjoys serving others

7. An encouraging person

8. Someone who prays

9. An organized person who is good at making plans

WAY TO SERVE

a. Planning a church activity or mission trip

b. Singing or playing music for the choir or praise team

c. Greeting and welcoming everyone to church

d. Tutoring students who need help at school

e. Talking with someone who feels sad or frustrated

f. Being a part of a prayer group that prays for people's needs

g. Counting up the money in the church offering plates

h. Cleaning up the church

i. Preparing meals to serve to people who don't have any food

Show Hospitality

1. Sit and talk with your guest	2. Fix a sleeping place
3. Pour juice	4. Put out cookies for 2 people
5. Offer a footwash	6. Bring hand sanitizer or a warm towel for hands.
7. Set the table	8. Clean up

Jesus, Mary, and Martha Cutouts

Luke 10:38–42

Unit 7

Opposition to Jesus

Lesson 29: Jesus Is Tempted

Activities

Map Activity: **Map of the Temptations of Jesus**
History Project: **Label Herod's Temple**
Craft Project: **Sand-dough Sculpture**
Memory Work: **Review the Twelve Disciples, Part I**
Coloring Page: **Jesus Is Tempted**

Map Activity

• •

Map of the Temptations of Jesus

Although the Bible does not give an exact location for the high mountain where the devil shows Jesus the kingdoms of the world, a probable location for this is the cliffs near Jericho, since you can see a panorama of the surrounding lands.

Materials

- Temptations map (Student Page 311)
- Temptation symbols (Student Page 313)
- Scissors
- Glue stick
- Pen or pencil
- Bible
- OPTIONAL: Coloring supplies

Directions

1 Read Matthew 4:1–11 aloud to the student.
2 Help the student cut out the temptation symbols on Student Page 313.
3 Tear out Student Page 311. Ask the student to find the Dead Sea on the map. Look south of it (below it) and you will see the desert region of the lower Jordan valley. (Today this desert area is called Wadi Arabah.)
4 Reread Matthew 4:1–4 aloud to the student. Ask, "What does the devil ask Jesus to do? Find the temptation symbol that shows this. Glue it on to the desert area (Wadi Arabah) on your map." *Answer: Turn stones into bread.*

5 Ask, "What is Jesus' response (verse 4)? I will help you write that next to the temptation symbol." *Answer: "Man does not live on bread alone, but on every word that comes from the mouth of God."*

6 Ask the student to find the city of Jerusalem on the map. This is where the temple was located.

7 Reread Matthew 4:5–7 aloud. Say, "What does the devil ask Jesus to do? Find the temptation symbol that shows this. Let's glue that symbol to the map." *Answer: "Throw yourself off the temple and the angels will catch you."*

8 Ask, "What is Jesus' response (verse 7)? I will help you write that next to the temptation symbol." *Answer: "Do not put the Lord your God to the test."*

9 Help the student find the city of Jericho. Say, "There are high cliffs here. If you stand on the top of one, you can see all the surrounding land. It is possible that the devil brought Jesus up here."

10 Reread Matthew 4:8–11. Say, "What does the devil offer Jesus? But what does Jesus have to do in exchange? Find the temptation symbol that shows this, and we'll glue it to your map." *Answer: The devil offers all the kingdoms of the world and their splendor to Jesus if he will only bow down and worship the devil.*

11 Tell the student, "Jesus says, 'Away from me, Satan!' What else does he say (verse 10)? I will help you write that next to the temptation symbol." *Answer: "Worship the Lord your God, and serve him only."*

12 The student may color the map.

History Project

· ·

Label Herod's Temple

Materials

- Diagram of Herod's Temple (Student Page 315)
- Colored pencils (purple, yellow, blue, orange, and green)

Directions

1 Read the following to the student, while showing the picture of Herod's Temple on Student Page 315:

The temple was the center of Jewish life, but by the time of Herod the Great (he was the king when Jesus was born) the temple was practically falling down. Herod decided to build a new, grander temple that would show what a great and powerful ruler he was. There was a lot to be done; the old temple was torn down and three valleys had to be filled with dirt to support the new structure. Huge walls had to be built to hold in the dirt. The temple itself was made of white marble that gleamed in the sunlight.

The temple was designed as a series of rectangles, one inside the other (like an onion that has outer and inner layers).

2 Tear out Student Page 315, and get out the colored pencils.
3 Point to the Court of the Gentiles, and describe it for the student while she colors the Court of the Gentiles purple (notice that it is on both sides of the temple):

The Court of the Gentiles was the outermost court of the temple. Jews and Gentiles (non-Jews) who believed in God could go there. The Gentiles could not go farther inside the temple. The Court of the Gentiles was filled with beggars and salesmen and money changers. It wasn't just a place of worship, and this angered Jesus (see Mark 11:15–17, for example).

4 Point to the Court of Women, and describe it for the student while she colors it yellow:

The next "layer" was the Court of Women. Jewish women and men could go in there. It was here that you could tithe your money. There was lots of singing and dancing in this court. This was as far as the women could go; only the men could go farther inside.

5 Point to the Court of the Israelites and describe it to the student while she colors it blue:

The next "layer" was the Court of the Israelites (the area between the steps and the altar). Only Jewish men could enter this area. From here the men could see the priests making sacrifices in the Court of the Priests.

6 Point to the Court of the Priests, and describe it to the student while she colors it orange:

This court was reserved for the priests. Here they would sacrifice animals on the altar before the white marble temple.

7 Point to the Temple, and describe it to the student while she colors it green:

Once you entered the temple, you would be in the Holy Place. Here you would see a gold altar where incense was burned day and night before the Lord, a table with twelve loaves of bread on it (to represent the twelve tribes of Israel), and a menorah (a stand with seven oil lamps that were kept burning all day and night). Beyond the Holy Place was a giant curtain. Behind the curtain was the Holy of Holies, where God was present in a special way. Only the High Priest was allowed to come in here, and he could only enter once a year. When Jesus died, the curtain in front of the Holy of Holies was torn in half (Mark 15:38).

Craft Project

. . . .

Sand-dough Sculpture

The sand-dough recipe at the bottom of this activity makes enough dough for 4 children. You can make it a day ahead and store it in a resealable sandwich bag. If you are doing this with a class, let them take home individual portions in sandwich bags.

Materials

- Sand dough (the recipe below makes enough for 4 students)
- Paper plate for each student
- Sandwich-size resealable baggie for each student
- OPTIONAL: Sand molds, shells, rocks (these items will be used if you have time for free play)

Directions

1 Give each student a portion of dough on a paper plate. Give the students a few minutes to handle and manipulate the dough.

2 Tell the students, "Jesus went to the desert to fast and pray. That's why this dough is sandy. What do you have a lot of in the desert? Sand. The devil came to Jesus in the desert and tempted him. The devil knew that Jesus was hungry. He told Jesus to turn the stones into bread. Shape your dough into a loaf of bread."

3 Say, "Jesus did not give into that temptation. He answered, 'Man does not live by bread alone but by every word that comes from the mouth of God.' So the devil tempted him again. He brought him to the top of the temple in Jerusalem. Shape your dough into a castle, because the temple was truly magnificent to look at. It was one of the most beautiful buildings in the world at that time."

4 Ask the students if they remember what the devil asked Jesus to do. (Answer: Throw himself off the top of the temple so the angels would catch him.) Tell them Jesus' answer: "Do not put the Lord your God to the test."

5 Say, "The devil tried to tempt Jesus again. He brought him to a mountaintop. Shape your dough into a mountain. What did the devil offer Jesus? (Answer: All the kingdoms and riches in the world.) But what did the devil want Jesus to do in return? (Answer: Worship him.) But Jesus answered, 'Worship the Lord your God and serve Him only.' Jesus did not give in to temptation."

6 If time allows, let the students play with the dough.

SAND-DOUGH RECIPE (MAKES ENOUGH FOR 4 STUDENTS)

Ingredients

- 4 c. fine sand
- 2 c. cornstarch
- 1 Tbsp. plus 1 tsp. cream of tartar
- 3 c. hot water
- Gallon-sized resealable bag

SAND-DOUGH DIRECTIONS

1 In a large saucepan, mix fine sand, cornstarch, and cream of tartar.
2 Stir in hot water.
3 Heat the saucepan on medium, stirring constantly until the water is absorbed and the mixture is quite difficult to stir. If the mixture is too wet, add a little more cornstarch. If it is too dry and crumbly, add more water.
4 Let dough cool. Knead it.
5 Store in a resealable bag. You can make this dough a day or so ahead of time.

Memory Work

. . . .

Review the Twelve Disciples, Part I

Directions

Say to the student, "You have already learned the names of six of the people who Jesus chose to learn from him and tell people about him. Let's review those names by saying them together, three times."

(Together, three times): Simon Peter, Andrew, James, John, Philip, Thomas.

Coloring Page

. . . .

Jesus Is Tempted

The devil took Jesus to the top of a mountain and showed him all the kingdoms of the world. He tried to trick Jesus into being selfish, and he said Jesus could have all these kingdoms if he didn't put God first. But Jesus would not do what the devil asked him to do. He obeyed God instead.

Temptations Map

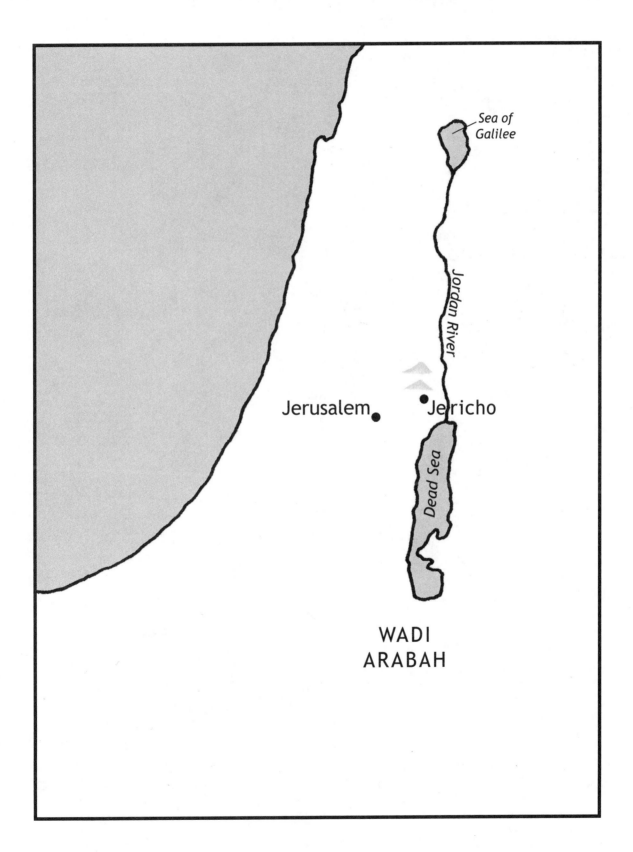

Sea of Galilee

Jordan River

Jerusalem

Jericho

Dead Sea

WADI
ARABAH

Temptation Symbols

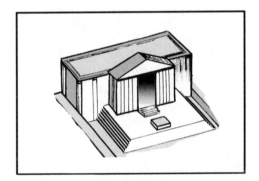

Herod's Temple

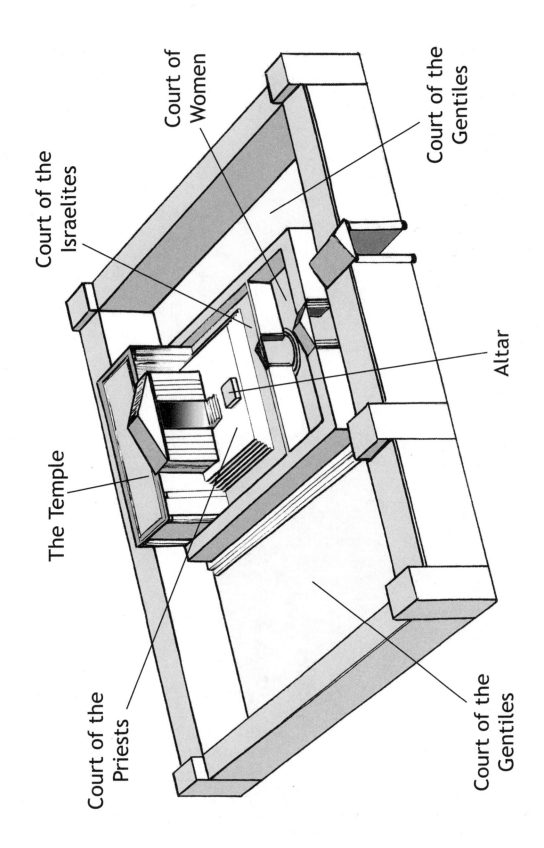

Court of Women

Court of the Gentiles

Court of the Israelites

Court of the Priests

The Temple

Altar

Court of the Gentiles

Matthew 4:1–11

Lesson 30: Jesus' Hometown Does Not Accept Him

Activities

Craft Project: **Build a Toolbox**
History Project: **Build a Synagogue**
Service Activity: **Learn Something New about a Person You Know**
Memory Work: **The Twelve Disciples, Part II**
Coloring Page: **Jesus' Hometown Does Not Accept Him**

Craft Project

· ·

Build a Toolbox

Jesus' father Joseph was a carpenter, or craftsman (Matthew 13:55), and Jesus probably learned from him how to do this kind of work. In this project the student will build his own small toolbox. This will be a bigger project than most in this book, and will require more time.
PLEASE NOTE that adult supervision is required for this project, as it involves "grown-up" tools.

Materials

- Wood glue
- Circular saw or jigsaw
- Hammer
- Sandpaper
- Saw
- Straight edge
- Tape measure
- Nails, 1"
- Wooden dowel, 1" diameter, at least 11" long
- Plywood or scrap wood, ½" thick
- Pencil

Directions

1   Have the student help you measure out two rectangles on the plywood to be the ends of the toolbox. Use 8 inches for the base measurement. This will make the "floor" of the

toolbox 7 inches wide when it is finished. Use a height of 10 inches for the rectangle. Show the student how to use a straight edge and pencil to mark the lines, and cut the two rectangles out using a jigsaw or circular saw.

2   Help the student measure the bottom and two sides of the toolbox. The bottom will go under the two sides and will be connected to the ends. The rectangular bottom should measure 8 inches by 11 inches, although you can shorten or lengthen this depending on your student and the size of the objects he'd like to keep in this box. Cut the sides. The sides will measure 3½ inches by 11 inches.

3   Measure 3½ inches from each corner on the top of the end pieces and have the student mark that spot. There should be 1 inch between the two marks on each end piece. Measure 4 inches up from each bottom corner on the end pieces and make a mark. In total, you should have four marks on each end, two on the top (1 inch apart) and one on each side 4 inches from the bottom.

4   Use a straight edge to draw a line connecting the point on the side to the point on the top and then for the other mark on the side to the other mark on the top. Do this on the other end piece as well. Cut along the lines you just made. When completed, the two ends should roughly resemble an upside-down letter V.

5   Using the saw, cut the dowel to 11 inches in length. This will be the handle of the toolbox.

6   Sand all surfaces, especially edges, so that the toolbox will not have harmful splinters.

7   Connect the base to the two ends. The base will fit inside the two ends, flush against the bottom. Help the student apply a line of wood glue along the ends of the base that will connect to the end pieces. Placing the base in a vise or supporting it by some other means, nail the ends to the base. They should be facing the same direction.

8   After nailing the ends to the base, connect the sides. The sides will fit between the ends and on top of the base. Apply wood glue to the three sides that will be connected to the ends and base. Nail the sides in place by nailing through the two ends into the sides first, and then, while applying pressure to the sides to keep them tight against the base, nail through the base into the sides.

9   Place the dowel at the top of the ends, where there is a 1-inch plateau. Apply glue to the two ends of the dowel and hold it securely in place between the two ends while nailing. Use two nails on each end for added stability.

10   Help the student wipe away any excess wood glue, and let the glue dry. Check to make sure that the toolbox will support the weight of some of the child's tools or toys.

History Project
· ·
Build a Synagogue

In Jesus' day, there was a synagogue in most towns in Galilee. A synagogue had some traditional elements. Build this basic model with a shoebox and Legos and other common supplies. If you want to make a more realistic-looking interior, you can use Styrofoam blocks (available at craft stores) painted brown or gray. These would take the place of the Legos.

Materials

- Shoebox
- Very small container of water (perhaps the plastic cap from a water bottle)
- Legos of assorted sizes
- Brown construction paper (2–3 sheets)
- Scissors
- Glue or tape
- OPTIONAL: Markers, glue stick, and sand/dirt

Directions

1   Have the student remove the lid from the shoebox and set the shoebox on its side with the open side facing him. This will be the synagogue. Tell the student that a synagogue was a building in the town for the people to worship and learn about God. The synagogues in Jesus' region, Galilee, were usually made of stone and built on the highest spot in the town.

2   Help the student cut the construction paper and attach it with the glue or tape to the inside of the shoebox. You may want to draw lines on the walls so the walls look like they are made of stone blocks.

3   OPTIONAL: You also may want to rub the glue stick on the ground and sprinkle the sand overtop. Shake off the excess sand. The floor of the synagogue was usually dirt. The common people of the town would bring mats and lay them on the floor to sit.

4   Tell the student that inside the synagogue, benches lined three of the walls. These benches were made of stone and were there for the important members of the town to sit upon. Usually, there were several rows of benches, but for our synagogue model, we will just have one row. Have the student build benches from the Legos and line them against the walls of the synagogue.

5   Tell the student that the benches all faced the center of the synagogue so the people could hear the rabbis and the readers that stood there. There was a raised platform for the rabbis (the teachers) and the people who would read the Scripture to stand on. There was also a menorah (a stand with seven oil lamps on it) on the platform. Have the student make a platform of Legos and place it in the center of the synagogue (or you can use a Lego "base" if you have one the right size).

6   There was one special seat called the Seat of Moses. During a synagogue service, the person who read from the Torah (the first five books of today's Bible) could sit in the seat since he was reading the words of Moses. (Moses was the writer of the Torah.) Have the student place a Lego brick near a wall to represent a chair.

7   Say to the student, "Outside the synagogue was a mikveh, a stone bath for the cleansing of people and objects before worship. The container of water will stand for our mikveh. Place it next to the synagogue."

8   Tell the student that the order of the service was usually this: Singing of a psalm, reading of the Shema (Deuteronomy 6:4–5), prayers, reading from the Scriptures, sermon by a rabbi, teacher, or townsperson, and a closing blessing. Read the Shema aloud ("Hear, O Israel: The LORD our God, the LORD is one. Love the LORD your God with all your heart and with all your soul and with all your strength") and imagine what it would be like to be in a synagogue in Jesus' time.

Service Activity

Learn Something New about a Person You Know

1 No one in Jesus' hometown of Nazareth knew that Jesus was a good teacher—they just thought he was a carpenter's son, so they didn't listen to him. There are probably lots of things you don't know about the people around you.

2 Ask your parents or grandparents about something you don't know about them. Ask things like:

a. What is something you are very good at? (Playing checkers? Making clay pots? Juggling? Playing the banjo? Speaking a different language?)

b. What do you remember about when you were in school? Has school changed much since you were my age? How has it changed?

c. What faraway places have you been to?

d. What is an interesting job that you've had?

Classroom Variation: If students are in a group, they can ask each other what they're good at—pair the students up with someone they may not know very well and ask them about talents they might have. Or have them interview the Sunday School teacher or pastor about what he or she does when not at church. Their teacher probably has all kinds of other talents and abilities outside of the classroom!

Memory Work

The Twelve Disciples, Part II

Materials

• The Twelve Disciples, Part II (Student Page 325)

Directions

Say to the student: "A few lessons ago, you learned the names of six of the twelve people who Jesus called to be his special helpers. Say those names with me now." *(Repeat the list of names twice through with the student: Simon Peter, Andrew, James, John, Philip, Thomas.)*

"Now here are the other six names. You will notice that there is another James in this second list. He had the same first name as the James we learned before, but he came from a different family, so we add his father's name in order to tell the two Jameses apart. We call him James the son of Alphaeus *[say AL-fee-uss]*."

"I will read this list two times: *(read these six names to the student twice)*: Matthew, James the son of Alphaeus *[say AL-fee-uss]*, Thaddeus, Simon, Judas, Bartholomew *(Bartholomew is also called Nathanael, as in the Bible story from this lesson.)*"

"Now let's repeat each of those names, so you'll know how to say them." *(Repeat each name with the student.)*

"Now let's see if we can say that list three times." *(Repeat list three times.)*

"Can you say all twelve names now? Let's try to say them together." *(Repeat the whole list with the student. She may not be able to remember all of them; don't push past the point of real frustration. Review the list each day.)*

Simon Peter, Andrew, James, John, Philip, Thomas, Matthew, James the son of Alphaeus, Thaddeus, Simon, Judas, Bartholomew (Nathanael).

Coloring Page

· ·

Jesus' Hometown Does Not Accept Him

Jesus came to teach in his hometown of Nazareth, but the people there didn't think he should teach them.

The Twelve Disciples, Part II

Simon Peter

Andrew

James

John

Philip

Thomas

Matthew

James the son of Alphaeus

Thaddeus

Simon

Judas

Bartholomew/Nathanael

Matthew 13:53–58

Lesson 31: Greater than Jonah and Solomon

Activities

Craft Project: **Make an Origami Fish**
Map Activity: **The Queen of Sheba's Journey**
Game Activity: **"Prove Yourself" Charades**
Service Activity: **Will They Notice Your Good Deeds?**
Memory Work: **Review the Twelve Disciples**
Coloring Page: **Jonah and the Big Fish**

Craft Project

• •

Make an Origami Fish

In the passage, Jesus refers to the prophet Jonah spending three days in the belly of a huge fish. Make this simple origami fish and ask the students, "What did Jesus say he had in common with Jonah?" (Answer: Just as Jonah spent three days in the belly of the fish, so Jesus will spend three days buried in the earth.")

Materials (for each student)

- Fish origami folding instructions (Student Page 333)
- 1 sheet of origami paper (available at craft stores) OR a piece of wrapping paper cut into a 6" x 6" square
- Pencil
- OPTIONAL: Wiggle eye and glue (wiggle eyes are available at Office Depot and at numerous online retailers)

Note to Instructor: Make your own origami fish along with the student since that is the easiest way for students to follow the directions.

Directions

1 Look at the folding diagrams on Student Page 333. Lay the piece of paper on the table, plain side up. The paper should be a diamond, with a corner pointing toward your belly. (Step 1)

2 Fold the paper in half to make a patterned triangle. Do this just to make the crease. Unfold the paper back to its original position. (Steps 2 & 3)

3 Now you will make a "kite" shape. Fold the right side into the center crease. Do the same with the left side. (Steps 4 & 5)

4 Fold the top of the "kite" down to meet the center of the kite. (Step 6)

5 Fold the entire fish in half, so only the patterned side of the paper shows. (Step 7)

6 Turn the fish on its side, flat part closest to you. (Step 8)

7 Fold up the tail of the fish along the line shown in the diagram. (Step 9)

8 Draw an eyeball on the fish, or glue on a wiggle eye. (Step 10) Now your fish is complete!

Map Activity

• •

The Queen of Sheba's Journey

The Queen of Sheba traveled from Yemen to Jerusalem by caravan. Help the student plot the journey with a road that represents all that she brought to Solomon.

Materials

- The Queen of Sheba's Journey map (Student Page 335)
- Pencil
- School glue
- Thin paintbrush or cotton swab
- 1 tsp. of each: sand, cinnamon, gold glitter, another glitter color (like red, blue, or green)
- Small bowl
- Bible

Directions

1 Read the account of the Queen of Sheba's visit to Solomon in 1 Kings 10:1–13. Ask the student if she can remember any of the gifts the Queen of Sheba gave Solomon. *Answer: She gave gold, precious stones, spices.*

2 Say, "The Queen of Sheba came to Jerusalem by caravan. What animal brought the loads of gifts she offered?" (Hint: These animals are still used to travel in the desert today.) *Answer: Camels brought the gifts.*

3 Say, "Jesus refers to the Queen of Sheba as the Queen of the South. She was likely from the south of the Arabian Peninsula, in the place where the country of Yemen is today." Ask the student to find Yemen on the map on Student Page 335. Assist her if necessary.

4 Say, "She traveled all the way from Yemen to the city of Jerusalem in Israel. Draw a line very lightly with the pencil from Yemen to Jerusalem."

5 Say "Remember, much of Arabia was desert. Add the sand to the small bowl."

6 Say, "The Queen brought a large amount of gold with her. Add the gold glitter to the bowl."

7 Say, "The Queen also brought precious stones. Add the colored glitter to the bowl."

8 Say, "The Queen brought spices as well. The Bible tells us no one had ever received so many spices as Solomon did from the Queen of Sheba. Add the cinnamon to the bowl." *Note to Instructor: Cinnamon is not a spice commonly grown in the Middle East, but we are*

using it in this project because it smells so good—better than cumin, turmeric, and oregano.

9   Help the student mix the contents of the bowl together.

10 Help the student squeeze a line of glue over the pencil line on her map. Have her use the paintbrush or cotton swab to make the line into a wide path.

11 Help her sprinkle the contents of the bowl onto the glue trail. Shake off any excess.

12 Let dry. If the student wants to, she can draw a picture of the queen's camel caravan along the route.

Game Activity

· ·

"Prove Yourself" Charades

The Pharisees demanded that Jesus prove himself, even though he had already done all kinds of things to show his authority. In this game, one person will try to convince the others that he or she is some person with power and authority.

Directions

1   Choose one person to act out the "authority figure." Whisper one of the roles below to that person, but don't let the other players hear!

2   Now that person has to act out the role, without speaking. We've provided some actions, but use your imagination to come up with more!

Prove You Are a King or Queen:
  Sit on a throne in a regal manner.
  Act out putting on a crown.

Prove You Are an Astronaut:
  Pretend to float, walk on the moon, and breathe through a helmet.

Prove You Are a Strong Man:
  Make muscles.
  Pretend to lift a big weight.

Pretend You Are a Police Officer:
  Pretend to blow a whistle, stop traffic, talk into a walkie-talkie.
  Drive quickly while making siren noises.
  Pretend to arrest someone.

Prove You Are a Boat Captain:
  Look through a telescope, steer a boat, order all hands on deck.
  Row.

Prove You Are a Parent:
  Take care of a baby doll, cook something.

3   The first person to guess what is being acted out becomes the next "actor."

Will They Notice Your Good Deeds?

Directions

1 Say to the student: "The people who demanded further signs from Jesus hadn't paid attention to all the miraculous things he had already said and done. Let's think of something good and kind we can do this week for someone we know. Let's see if they notice what we do."

2 Help the student think of something kind she can do, every day for a week, for a sibling or parent. *Suggestions: always pick up this person's clothes, feed pets, take out garbage, compliment them every day, set the table without complaining, let them have the last cookie/piece of cake, every day ask your parent one time, "Can I help?"*

3 Make sure the student does her kind deed every day this week, quietly reminding her if necessary. You may want to tip off the recipient about what is going on, towards the end of the week, if you feel the student needs encouragement.

Memory Work

Review the Twelve Disciples

If you still have the Student Page with all the names on it from Lesson 30 (Student Page 325), you can use it as an aid in this review. Try covering up one or two of the names, increasing the number until the student can say the names without seeing any of them.

Directions

Say to the student: "You have learned the names of all twelve of Jesus' disciples. First you learned six of them, starting with Simon Peter. Let's say those six together, three times."

(Together, 3 times): Simon Peter, Andrew, James, John, Philip, Thomas.

"Good! Then you learned another group of six, starting with Matthew. Let's say those together three times."

(Together, 3 times): Matthew, James the son of Alphaeus, Thaddeus, Simon, Judas, Bartholomew (Nathanael).

"Let's try to say the whole list together now, with all twelve names."

(Together): Simon Peter, Andrew, James, John, Philip, Thomas, Matthew, James the son of Alphaeus, Thaddeus, Simon, Judas, Bartholomew (Nathanael).

Coloring Page

Jonah and the Big Fish

In today's lesson, Jesus talked about Jonah who was thrown into the sea and swallowed by a giant fish!

Fish Origami

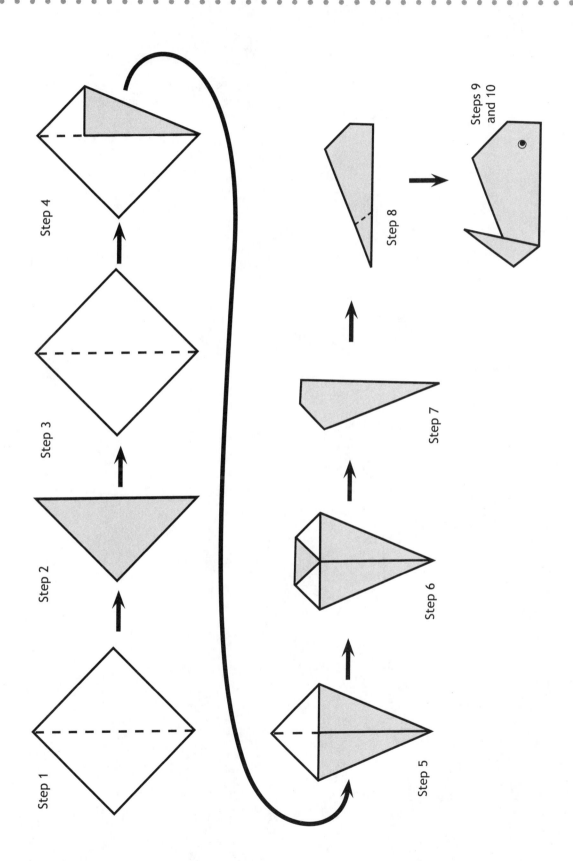

Step 1

Step 2

Step 3

Step 4

Step 5

Step 6

Step 7

Step 8

Steps 9 and 10

Queen of Sheba's Journey Map

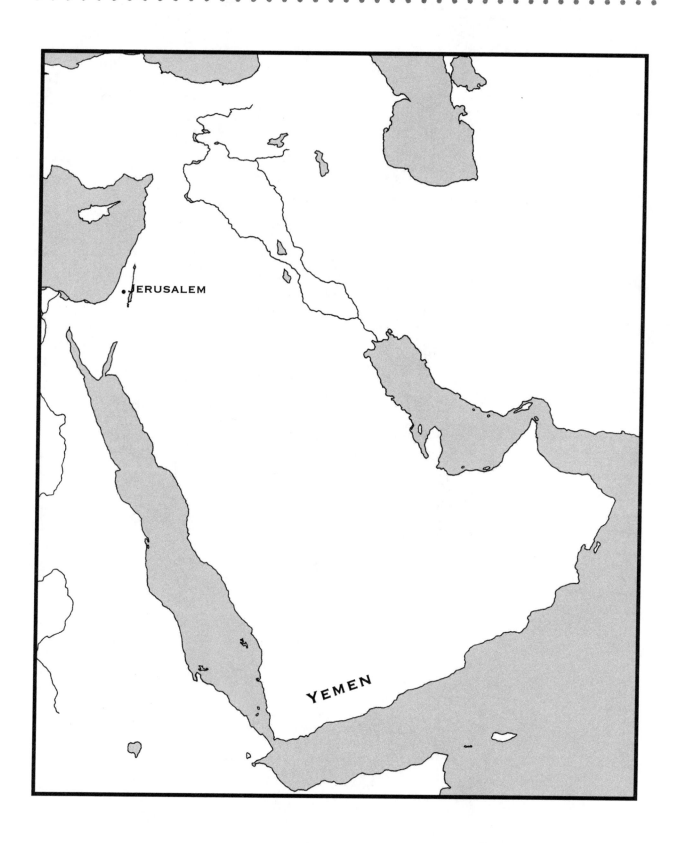

JERUSALEM

YEMEN

Matthew 12:38-42

Lesson 32: Jesus' Time Had Not Yet Come

Activities

Game Activity: **"What Were They Saying about Jesus?" Secret Code**
Game Activity: **Hide!**
Craft Project: **Make a Booth for the Feast of the Tabernacles**
Science Activity: **Appearing Ink—Realizing Who Jesus Is**
Memory Work: **Review the Twelve Disciples**
Coloring Page: **The Crowd Is Angry with Jesus**

Game Activity

. . . .

"What Were They Saying about Jesus?" Secret Code

The student looks at all the things people in the crowd were saying about Jesus and chooses one to change into a code for the instructor or a fellow student to decode.

Materials (for each student)

- "What Were They Saying about Jesus?" code sheet (Student Pages 343 and 344)
- Pencil
- Scissors

Directions

1 Turn to Student Pages 343 and 344. The first step is for the student to come up with a code. Fill in the code boxes with the alphabet in mixed-up order. Tell the student to do this at random. Write "A" in one box (over the letter V, for example) and "B" in another box (over the letter J, for example). Keep doing this until the student has run through all the letters in the alphabet and all the boxes are filled.

2 The student should pick one of the things the people in the crowd were saying about Jesus. He should not tell anyone what he is picking.

3 Using his code boxes as a key, the student should write the corresponding code letter over each letter in the saying he has chosen.

4 Once this is done, the student should rewrite ONLY the code letters on the bottom half of the sheet.

5   The student should cut out his code and his secret code saying and give it to the instructor or to a fellow student, who will then use the code boxes to write the correct letters over the saying and decode it.

6   Ask the student how Jesus responds to the people's questions and accusations. Read his response to him again: "Yes, you know me, and you know where I am from. I am not here on my own, but he who sent me is true. You do not know him, but I know him because I am from him and he sent me."

7   If time allows, the student should use the code he created to write a short message for a friend to decode.

Game Activity

Hide!

The angry crowd tried to grab Jesus, but they could not, because God had more for him to do. Jesus somehow hid himself from the crowd or kept them from grabbing him. This fun game for groups, essentially the game of Sardines, reinforces that idea, though of course no one is trying to beat up your student! The game is best played indoors in the dark but can be played in the daytime too.

Directions

1   Choose one student to be the hidden person. He or she hides somewhere while all the other players count to 40.

2   When the other players have finished counting, have them scatter and try to find the hiding player. Whenever a player finds the hider, that player should hide with the hider. When someone else finds those two, that person will join them in hiding, and so on, until everyone has found the hiding spot.

3   Remind the students that as more and more people find the hiders, the hiding group should try to stay quiet and not whisper or giggle, or else they will be found too easily!

4   When this round of the game is over, let the first student who found the hidden person become the hider for the next round.

Craft Project

Make a Booth for the Feast of the Tabernacles

Jesus was at the temple in Jerusalem for the Feast of the Tabernacles, called Sukkot *in Hebrew. Sukkot is the plural of* sukkah, *which means "tabernacle" or "booth." Learn a little about Sukkot, and make a "booth," which is one of the ways the Jews observe this holiday.*

Materials

- Furniture (sofa, chairs, tables—whatever you use to make a fort)
- 2–3 sheets green poster board (for the branches, or use real branches)
- Pencil

- Scissors
- Sheets or blankets
- Snack to eat inside the *sukkah*

Directions

1 Tell the student about *Sukkot*: "There are three festivals in the Jewish religion in which the people living in Israel were expected to travel to the temple in Jerusalem. These were the Passover, Festival of Weeks (Shavuot), and the Feast of the Tabernacles (Sukkot). God told the Israelites when to celebrate Sukkot. It is a seven-day festival to celebrate the bringing in of the fruit harvest. It begins on the 15th day of the month of Tishrei on the Jewish calendar, which means it happens during September or October. The word *Sukkot* means 'tents' or 'booths.' God told the Israelites to build booths and live in them during the festival to remember that when God led them out of Egypt, they lived in such places (Leviticus 23:42–43)."

2 Build your own version of a sukkah (booth). The Israelites were told by God to build them out of hadar trees, leafy branches, palm branches, and willows (Leviticus 23:40). Today Jewish families build their *sukkot* in front of their houses and eat all their meals in them (some families even sleep in them). Gather your furniture in a cluster and drape sheets and blankets over the furniture to create a booth inside. Don't forget to enclose the ceiling!

3 Cut long leaf, palm, and branch shapes from the poster board (you may wish to sketch these with a pencil before you cut them out—use the palm branch template from Lesson 33, Student Page 353 and enlarge it). Or use real branches from trees and bushes in your yard. Drape these leaves and branches over the roof of the sukkah.

4 Take a snack to eat in your *sukkah* and enjoy!

Science Activity

• •

Appearing Ink—Realizing Who Jesus Is

Materials

- Small cup of lemon juice (do not use lemonade)
- Blank paper
- Small paintbrush, such as you would use for watercolor paints

Directions

1 Dip the paintbrush in the lemon juice, and use it to write on the paper one of Jesus' miracles that has been covered in Lessons 6–10.
   Options: Turned water into wine; stopped a storm; fed many people; walked on water; healed a centurion's servant.

2 Set the paper aside for several minutes, until the lemon juice is completely dry.

3 Help the student hold the paper an inch or two above a hot lightbulb (100-watt works well). Do not place the paper directly on the bulb!

4   The name of the miracle should begin to appear as the lemon juice oxidizes and turns brown.

5   Talk about how seeing the miracles made some people begin to believe that Jesus was someone very special. Other people saw the miracles but didn't understand who he was.

Memory Work
. . . .
Review the Twelve Disciples

If you still have the Student Page with all the names on it, from Lesson 30 (Student Page 325), you can use it as an aid in this review. Try covering up one or two of the names, increasing the number until the student can say the names without seeing any of them.

Directions

Say to the student: "You have learned the names of all twelve of Jesus' disciples. First you learned six of them, starting with Simon Peter. Let's say those six together, three times."

(Together, three times): Simon Peter, Andrew, James, John, Philip, Thomas.

"Good! Then you learned another group of six, starting with Matthew. Let's say those together three times."

(Together, three times): Matthew, James the son of Alphaeus, Thaddeus, Simon, Judas, Bartholomew (Nathanael).

"Let's try to say the whole list together now, with all twelve names."

(Together): Simon Peter, Andrew, James, John, Philip, Thomas, Matthew, James the son of Alphaeus, Thaddeus, Simon, Judas, Bartholomew (Nathanael).

Coloring Page
. . . .
The Crowd Is Angry with Jesus

While he was teaching at the temple, Jesus said that God had sent him. Some people were angry that he said this. They tried to grab him to hurt him, but they could not, because he still had more to do and to say.

What Were They Saying about Jesus?

Code:

☐☐☐☐☐☐☐☐☐☐☐☐☐☐☐☐☐☐☐☐☐☐☐☐☐☐

Ⓐ Ⓑ Ⓒ Ⓓ Ⓔ Ⓕ Ⓖ Ⓗ Ⓘ Ⓙ Ⓚ Ⓛ Ⓜ Ⓝ Ⓞ Ⓟ Ⓠ Ⓡ Ⓢ Ⓣ Ⓤ Ⓥ Ⓦ Ⓧ Ⓨ Ⓩ

Choose a saying to write in code:

☐☐☐☐ ☐☐☐☐ ☐☐ ☐☐☐☐ ☐☐☐☐
T H E Y   W A N T   T O   K I L L   T H I S

☐☐☐ .
M A N .

☐☐☐☐ ☐☐☐ ☐☐☐ ☐☐☐☐☐☐ ☐
T H E Y   A R E   N O T   S A Y I N G   A

☐☐☐☐ ☐☐ ☐☐☐ .
W O R D   T O   H I M .

☐☐ ☐☐ ☐☐☐☐☐☐☐☐ ☐☐ ☐☐☐☐☐☐ .
H E   I S   S P E A K I N G   I N   P U B L I C .

☐☐ ☐☐☐☐ ☐☐☐☐☐ ☐☐ ☐☐
D O   T H E Y   T H I N K   H E   I S

☐☐☐ ☐☐☐☐☐☐ ?
T H E   C H R I S T ?

☐☐ ☐☐☐☐ ☐☐☐☐☐ ☐☐
W E   K N O W   W H E R E   H E

☐☐ ☐☐☐☐ .
I S   F R O M .

☐☐ ☐☐☐ ☐☐☐☐ ☐☐☐☐ ☐☐☐☐☐
N O   O N E   W I L L   K N O W   W H E R E

☐☐☐ ☐☐☐☐☐☐ ☐☐ ☐☐☐☐ .
T H E   C H R I S T   I S   F R O M .

☐ ☐☐☐☐☐☐☐ ☐☐ ☐☐ ☐☐☐
I   B E L I E V E   H E   I S   T H E

☐☐☐☐☐☐☐ .
M E S S I A H .

Secret Code to Decode:

John 7:25–31

John 1:2-3

Unit 8

The End of Jesus' Life

Lesson 33: Jesus Rides into Jerusalem as a King

Activities

Craft Activity: **Make a Palm Branch**
Music Activity: **Learn the *Sanctus***
Art History Project: Giotto's *Entry into Jerusalem*
Art Project: **Create a Fresco-style Painting like Giotto's *Entry into Jerusalem***
Memory Work: **Review the Twelve Disciples**
Coloring Page: Jesus Rides into Jerusalem

Craft Project

· ·

Make a Palm Branch

Materials

- Palm template (Student Page 353)
- Scissors
- 1 piece of green construction paper per student
- 1 green pipe cleaner per student
- 1 pencil or marker per student
- Scotch tape

Directions

1 Say to the student, "When Jesus rode into Jerusalem, the crowds celebrated and made a parade! They cut branches from the trees and waved them in the air, to welcome him. Today we'll make our own palm-tree branch to wave."
2 Cut out the palm template on Student Page 353.
3 Have the student trace the template onto the green construction paper and cut it out.
4 Tape the green pipe cleaner to the center of the palm leaf.

Learn the *Sanctus*

Learn the Sanctus, *a component of many Christian church services and the Latin translation of "Hosanna in the highest! Blessed is he who comes in the name of the Lord!"*

Materials

- *Sanctus* (Student Page 355)
- Sound recording of choral version of *Sanctus**

*Sanctus has been a part of Christian liturgies for centuries, and as a result several notable composers have set it to music: Beethoven, Haydn, Bach, Schubert, and Mozart, to name a few. Search your library or an online music source for some of these recordings that the students can listen to. Another good option is www.youtube.com. Just search under "Sanctus" plus the composer's name, and you'll find several. If you want to hear a more unusual version, try to find the Sanctus *from the* Missa Luba *(released in 1965 in the U.S.), in which a Congolese children's choir and a Belgian priest arranged the traditional Christian liturgy in Congolese style.*

Directions

1 Read the students the English version of *Sanctus*. Point out to the students that the words in bold print are the words that the people shouted as Jesus rode into Jerusalem. If the students go to a church where the *Sanctus* is not spoken or said every week, tell them that in some churches people say this every week as a way of praising Jesus.

Holy, Holy, Holy
Lord God of Hosts
Heaven and earth are full of your glory
Hosanna in the highest
Blessed is he who comes in the name of the Lord
Hosanna in the highest

2 Now read the Sanctus in Latin. Tell the students that in the Catholic church, the whole church service used to be in this language. Point out to them that the words in bold mean "Hosanna in the highest! Blessed is he who comes in the name of the Lord! Hosanna in the highest!" "Hosanna" means "save!" Can they find the word "Hosanna" and point to it?

Sanctus, Sanctus, Sanctus (SAHNK toos)

Dominus Deus Sabaoth (DOM ee noos DAY oos SAH bah ohth)

Pleni sunt caeli et terra gloria tua (PLEH ni soont CHEH lee et TAIR uh GLOR ee ah TOO ah)

***Hosanna in excelsis** (Hoh SAH nah in ek SHELL sees)*

***Benedictus qui venit in nomine Domini** (beh neh DIK toos quee VEH neet in NOH mee nay DOH mih nee)*

***Hosanna in excelsis** (Hoh SAH nah in ek SHELL sees)*

3 Choose one of the sound recordings of *Sanctus* (pick the shortest one). Tell the students to listen carefully and put their finger on their nose when they hear the choir sing "Hosanna." Play the recoding.

4 If your church sings a version of the *Sanctus* in English or Latin (or any other language), sing it with the students while they wave the palm branches they made in the previous activity.

Art History Project

· ·

Giotto's *Entry into Jerusalem*

Giotto di Bondone, the father of the Italian Renaissance, did a series of frescoes on the life of Christ in the Arena Chapel in Padua. This one depicts the scene from the lesson: Jesus' entry into Jerusalem. The student will learn a little bit about fresco painting, and in the next project she will make her own fresco depicting this Palm Sunday scene.

Materials

- Image of Giotto's *Entry into Jerusalem* (Student Page 357, but see it in color at www.artres. com, where you can find it easily if you search for "Giotto Jerusalem")

Directions

Show the student the painting as you say the following. Encourage her to answer the questions in complete sentences.

1 This painting was created by Giotto di Bondone, who lived seven hundred years ago. According to one old story, Giotto was a shepherd boy from a town near Florence, Italy. One day young Giotto was drawing the sheep he was looking after when a famous artist walked by. He saw Giotto's drawing and immediately noticed the boy's talent. After that, Giotto became one of his students. Another story says that Giotto's teacher went on an errand and left Giotto alone in his art studio. Giotto painted a fly on his teacher's painting. When the teacher returned, he thought the fly was real and tried to swat it off!

2 As Giotto got older, he became well known as a skilled painter. In 1305, he was asked to paint frescoes on the walls of a church in the town of Padua, in Italy. Giotto painted 37 scenes from the life of Mary and the life of Jesus. He painted differently from the other painters of his time: the people looked more real and more natural. Their faces had expression and showed emotion, and their clothes hung on them the way real clothes do. Because of the way the people stand and are arranged in the painting, the person looking at the painting feels like she is a part of the scene. All this was a new way of painting, and Giotto influenced many painters who came after him.

3 Look at Giotto's fresco about the event from this week's lesson, when Jesus came to Jerusalem. (Show the student the picture of the fresco.) A fresco is a type of painting done on wet plaster, the stuff that walls used to be coated with (if you live in an old house, your walls are probably plaster). This fresco is one of the scenes from the life of Jesus that Giotto painted on the walls of the church. It is called *Entry into Jerusalem* and it shows Jesus arriving in Jerusalem. Do you see how the crowd is welcoming him? They are waving branches, and some are taking off their coats for Jesus' donkey to walk on.

4   Now I will ask you some questions. Think back to the story from the lesson. Now look at the painting. Which one is Jesus? How can you tell? (He is the one riding a donkey.)

5   Behind Jesus and the disciples are men in trees. What are they doing up there? (Pulling down palm branches.)

6   Can you find someone in the crowd waving a palm branch? (He is a young boy standing near the head of the donkey.)

7   Look at the man standing in front of the boy. You can't see his face because it is covered up. What is he doing? (He is taking off his cloak.)

8   Why is the man taking off his cloak? Hint: Look at the man kneeling in front of him. (They are laying their cloaks down in front of Jesus for the donkey to walk on.)

9   There is a building behind the people. What do you think this place is? Remember the story and where Jesus is going. (It is Jerusalem.)

10 Do you remember what the people were shouting? [If the student does not remember, you can reread Matthew 21:9: "The crowds that went ahead of him and those that followed shouted, 'Hosanna to the Son of David!' 'Blessed is he who comes in the name of the Lord!' 'Hosanna in the highest!'"] (Hosanna to the Son of David! OR Blessed is he who comes in the name of the Lord! OR Hosanna in the highest!)

Art Project

. . . .

Create a Fresco-style Painting like Giotto's *Entry into Jerusalem*

Materials

- Box or tub of plaster of paris mix (available at hardware stores and at Amazon.com)
- Small aluminum foil pan
- Water
- Watercolor paints and brushes
- Plastic spoon and mixing bowl
- Planned drawing to be painted

Directions

1   Fresco painting requires accuracy because you cannot correct any mistakes you might make. So for best results, have the student plan out her design and color choices on paper first.

2   Follow the directions on the box of plaster of paris to create the plaster mix. Quickly pour the plaster into a small aluminum foil pan. Have the student use the back of a plastic spoon to smooth the surface of the plaster. *Please note: You should NEVER pour liquid plaster down the sink or wash items that have plaster on them in the sink! Plaster can set under water and will clog your pipes!*

3   When the plaster is firm but still damp to the touch, it is ready to be painted.

4   Have the student paint her picture onto the plaster with watercolors. As the plaster dries, the pigments from the paint will be permanently set into the plaster.

5   When the plaster has completely dried, remove the tile from the pan and display.

Memory Work

. . . .

Review the Twelve Disciples

If you still have the Student Page with all the names on it, from Lesson 30 (Student Page 325) you can use it as an aid in this review. Try covering up one or two of the names, increasing the number until the student can say the names without seeing any of them.

Directions

Say to the student: "You have learned the names of all twelve of Jesus' disciples. First you learned six of them, starting with Simon Peter. Let's say those six together, three times."

(Together, three times): Simon Peter, Andrew, James, John, Philip, Thomas.

"Good! Then you learned another group of six, starting with Matthew. Let's say those together three times."

(Together, three times): Matthew, James the son of Alphaeus, Thaddeus, Simon, Judas, Bartholomew (Nathanael).

"Let's try to say the whole list together now, with all twelve names."

(Together): Simon Peter, Andrew, James, John, Philip, Thomas, Matthew, James the son of Alphaeus, Thaddeus, Simon, Judas, Bartholomew (Nathanael).

Coloring Page

. . . .

Jesus Rides into Jerusalem

When Jesus came to the city of Jerusalem, the people celebrated because they knew God had sent him. They waved palm branches and cheered for him. But he didn't ride in on a war horse, like a king would do. He rode on an ordinary donkey.

Palm Template

Sanctus

Holy, Holy, Holy
Lord God of Hosts
Heaven and earth are full of your glory
Hosanna in the highest
Blessed is he who comes in the name of the Lord
Hosanna in the highest

Sanctus, Sanctus, Sanctus
Dominus Deus Sabaoth
Pleni sunt caeli et terra gloria tua
Hosanna in excelsis
Benedictus qui venit in nomine Domini
Hosanna in excelsis

Entry into Jerusalem by Giotto

Scala/Art Resource, NY

Matthew 21:1–11

Lesson 34: A Fig Tree

Activities

Science Activity: **Learn about the Fig**
Cooking Project: **Fig Bars**
Game Activity: **Fig Maze**
Memory Work: **Review the Books of the New Testament**
Coloring Page: **Jesus and the Fig Tree**

Science Activity

• •

Learn about the Fig

Test the student's listening skills as he learns about the fig tree and colors a page of pictures.

Materials

- Fig and fig tree pictures (Student Page 365, with five pictures)
- Colored pencils or crayons

Directions

1   Turn to the fig tree pictures (Student Page 365). Read each of the following sentences to the student and have him follow the instructions to fill in the correct answer.
2   The fig tree can grow to be up to thirty feet tall. Color the picture of the fig tree. In the blank below the fig tree, write how tall the fig tree can grow.
3   The leaves are large—they can be as big as 7 inches wide and 10 inches tall. That is twice as big as your hand. Color the leaf a deep green. Circle the right answer: Are fig leaves big or small?
4   The fruit is 1 or 2 inches long. It is green, but as it ripens it turns purple-brown. Color the cluster of figs the color of a ripe fig.
5   The fruit is sweet, and the inside of the fig fruit isn't smooth like the inside of an apple or a pear. This is because the fig tree has no visible flowers (usually, fruit trees grow flowers first and then develop the fruit). But the fig fruit contains the flower inside it. The fig is called a false fruit, because the fruit is really made of the flowers and the seeds mixed together. Color the picture of a fig fruit split in half. Color the seeds green and the inside flesh of the fruit pink and white.

6 One variety of the fig has a small opening at the top for a particular wasp, called the fig wasp, to climb inside and pollinate the hidden flower. Color the picture of the fig wasp. Draw a line from the fig wasp to a fig fruit.

Cooking Project

Fig Bars

Figs are excellent sources of calcium, potassium, and fiber. While fresh figs are delicious, they are hard to transport, so you rarely see them in a grocery store. Dried figs are abundant, however. Try this recipe to make your own version of Fig Newtons.

Ingredients

- 1 c. water
- 3 c. dried figs, chopped
- ½ c. honey
- 1 c. sugar
- 1 stick butter, softened
- 1 Tbsp. milk
- 1 tsp. vanilla
- 1¾ c. flour
- 1 tsp. baking powder
- ½ tsp. cinnamon
- ½ tsp. salt

Directions

1 Have the student put the figs and water in a small saucepan. DO NOT HEAT. Let them sit in the water for 1 hour.
2 Help the student add honey to the figs and water, and then show him how to stir the saucepan over medium heat. Let him stir until the mixture is thick like jam (about 10 minutes). If you want the fig mixture to be smoother, let him mash it with a potato masher. Then leave the mixture to sit until it is cool.
3 Preheat the oven to 350 degrees F. Have the student help you grease a 9" x 13" pan. In a large mixing bowl, use an electric mixer to cream the butter and sugar. The student can do this if you feel comfortable letting him use the mixer. Have the student add the milk and the vanilla. Then have him mix in the flour, baking powder, cinnamon, and salt.
4 Divide the dough in half. Roll out half of the dough on a floured surface until it is about 9" x 13". Have the student place that half of the dough on the bottom of the greased pan.
5 Let the student help you pour the fig filling over the dough.
6 Roll out the second half of the dough until it is 9" x 13." Help the student lay the second half of the dough over the fig mixture,
7 Bake 25–30 minutes until golden. Let cool and cut into bars.

Game Activity

•••

Fig Maze

The inside of a fig is actually the fig flower. (It even looks pretty maze-like in there!) See if the student can find his way out.

Materials

- Fig Maze (Student Page 367)
- Pencil

Directions

Have the student use a pencil to navigate through the fig.

Memory Work

•••

Review the Books of the New Testament

Directions

Say to the student: "You have learned all of the books of the New Testament! Let's review them all to make sure they stay in your memory. The first five were Matthew, Mark, Luke, John, and Acts. Let's say those together."

[Together]: Matthew, Mark, Luke, John, Acts.

"Then we learned nine more books, the letters that Paul wrote to different groups of people. They were Romans, First and Second Corinthians, Galatians, Ephesians, Philippians, Colossians, First and Second Thessalonians. Let's say those together."

[Together]: Romans, First and Second Corinthians, Galatians, Ephesians, Philippians, Colossians, First and Second Thessalonians.

"Then we learned four more books, the letters Paul sent to specific people. Let's say those together."

[Together]: First and Second Timothy, Titus, Philemon.

"The last set of books was written to different churches and people as messages by God, by different writers. They were Hebrews, James, First and Second Peter, First, Second, and Third John, Jude, Revelation. Let's say those names together three times."

[Together, three times]: Hebrews, James, First and Second Peter, First, Second, and Third John, Jude, Revelation.

• •

Jesus and the Fig Tree

This fig tree looked like a good tree, but it wasn't producing any fruit. Just like that tree, some people in Jesus' time were saying they liked Jesus, but weren't doing anything to show it. Jesus made the tree wither. This was to show people that they needed to do the right things and not just talk about doing them.

Fig Pictures

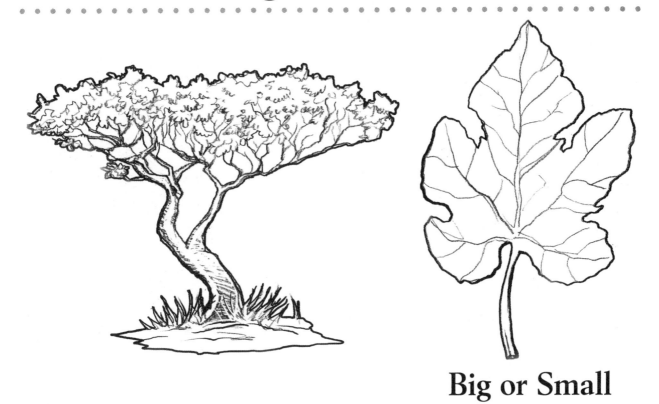

Big or Small

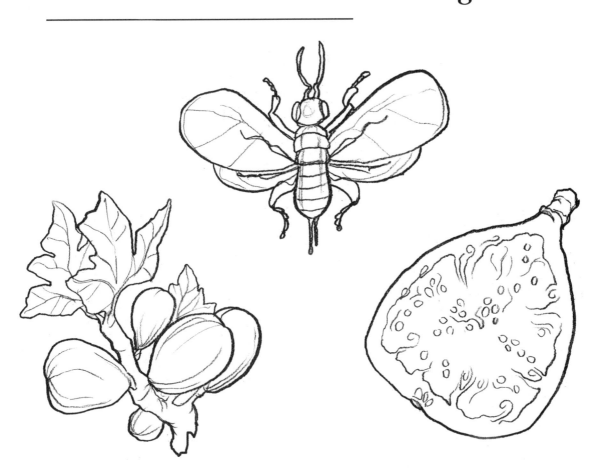

Fig Maze

Start at the stem.

Find your way through the fruit

to the star in the center of the fig!

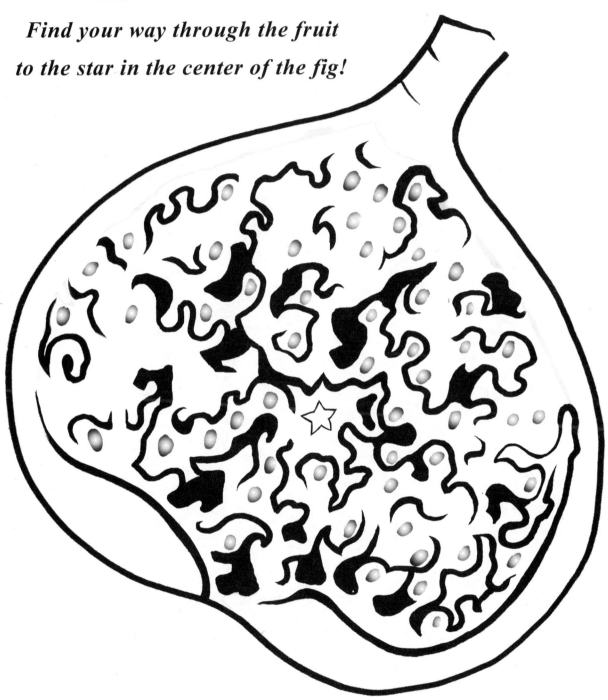

Matthew 21:18–22

Lesson 35: Jesus Outsmarts the Religious Leaders

Activities

History Project: **Who Was John the Baptist?**
Art Project: **John the Baptist Picture with Classic Elements**
Cooking Project: **Eat a "Locust" and Honey**
Memory Work: **Say the Names of the Twelve Disciples to an Audience**
Coloring Page: **John Baptizes People**

History Project

• •

Who Was John the Baptist?

These questions should be asked and answered orally. Help the students find out more about John the Baptist by reading specific Bible passages.

Materials

- None

Directions

1 Say, "In this week's lesson, Jesus talks about John the Baptist to the religious leaders in the temple. Let's find out more about this person, John. I will ask you something about John the Baptist, and then I'll read to you a Bible verse that contains the answer. Listen carefully and see if you can hear it."

2 Ask, "Who were John's parents?" Read Luke 1:13: "But the angel said to him: 'Do not be afraid, Zechariah; your prayer has been heard. Your wife Elizabeth will bear you a son, and you are to give him the name John.'"
Answer: Zechariah and Elizabeth.

3 Ask, "What kind of clothing did John wear?" Read Matthew 3:4: "John's clothes were made of camel's hair, and he had a leather belt around his waist. His food was locusts and wild honey."
Answer: Clothes of camel hair and a leather belt.

4 Ask, "What did he eat?" (This answer is included in the verse you read for Question 3, but if necessary, read Matthew 3:4 again: "John's clothes were made of camel's hair, and

he had a leather belt around his waist. His food was locusts and wild honey.")
Answer: He ate locusts and honey.

5   Ask, "What did John say that his voice was calling?" Read John 1:23: "John replied in the words of Isaiah the prophet, 'I am the voice of one calling in the desert, "Make straight the way for the Lord."'"
Answer: "Make straight the way for the Lord!"

6   Ask, "What was John doing to the people who were confessing their sins?" Read Mark 1:4–5: "And so John came, baptizing in the desert region and preaching a baptism of repentance for the forgiveness of sins. The whole Judean countryside and all the people of Jerusalem went out to him. Confessing their sins, they were baptized by him in the Jordan River."
Answer: He was baptizing them with water.

7   Ask, "Where was John baptizing the people?" Read Mark 1:5 again: "The whole Judean countryside and all the people of Jerusalem went out to him. Confessing their sins, they were baptized by him in the Jordan River."
Answer: He baptized them in the Jordan River.

8   Say, "John said that there was one person he was not worthy to baptize. Who was that person?" Read John 1:26–30: " 'I baptize with water,' John replied, 'but among you stands one you do not know. He is the one who comes after me, the thongs of whose sandals I am not worthy to untie.' This all happened at Bethany on the other side of the Jordan, where John was baptizing. The next day John saw Jesus coming toward him and said, 'Look, the Lamb of God, who takes away the sin of the world! This is the one I meant when I said, "A man who comes after me has surpassed me because he was before me."'"
Answer: Jesus.

9   Ask, "What happened to John?" Read Luke 3:20: "Herod added this to all the evil things he had done: he threw John in prison."
Answer: Herod threw him in jail.

Art Project

· ·

John the Baptist Picture with Classic Elements

After the student has answered the questions in the previous activity, have him draw a picture of John the Baptist, wearing his unusual clothes and baptizing people in the River Jordan.

Materials

- White paper
- Pencil
- Crayons, colored pencils, or markers
- Bible

Directions

1   Tell the student about how John the Baptist is traditionally portrayed in works of art. John is often shown as a thin man (due to his strict diet), with a long hair and beard, wearing furs or animal skins. Sometimes he is shown pointing up to heaven to symbolize

his ministry of calling people to turn back to God. Sometimes a lamb is with him because he called Jesus "the lamb of God" in John 1:29. You can see one example of this in Titian's 16th-century painting of John, which can be found at http://en.wikipedia.org/wiki/File:Titian-John_the_Baptist.jpg.

2 Have the student draw a picture of John the Baptist with the pencil. See if she can include:
>   John's messy hair and beard
>   A fur outfit (of camel hair or sheepskin)
>   John pointing to heaven to tell people about God
>   A lamb
>   The Jordan River, where John baptized people who were turning from their sinful ways

Cooking Project
. . . .
Eat a "Locust" and Honey

Ingredients

- 1 banana
- 3 cheese sticks
- 1 piece of bread (the end piece)
- 1 marshmallow
- Peanut butter
- Chocolate chips OR peanut-butter chips
- 1 of any kind of nut
- 1 piece of uncooked spaghetti OR 2 pieces of long thin candy (licorice, etc.)
- Honey
- OPTIONAL: Jelly or jam of any kind

Read Mark 1:6 to the student. Then say, "Today we're going to make locusts and wild honey so we can eat what John the Baptist ate while he lived out in the desert. A locust is a kind of grasshopper."

1 Have the student peel a banana. This will be the locust's body. The end of the banana that curves is the locust's rear; the straight end is the head. The curved end (rear) should be pointing up.
2 Help the student cut off the very tip of the straight end of the banana (about half an inch). Help the student cut a marshmallow in half, then let him use peanut butter to stick the half-marshmallow to the front of the banana. This is the head. The student can also use peanut-butter chips or chocolate chips for eyes and a nut for the mouth. These can all be stuck to the marshmallow with peanut butter. You may have to cut the nut a little to fit, depending on what kind you use; the adult should do this since a knife sharp enough to cut a nut could be dangerous. The antennae can be a piece of uncooked spaghetti snapped in half or any kind of long thin candy stuck into the marshmallow.
3 Help the student cut one of the cheese sticks in half end to end, then again side to side.

These four pieces of cheese can be stuck onto the sides of the banana near the marshmallow head, flat side down, with peanut butter. There should be two small legs on each side. The two larger back legs are another two cheese sticks. Help the student cut them about half-way through horizontally, but make sure they're not cut all the way. Bend them into V shapes and peanut butter them near the curved end of the banana, with the points of the V facing up.

4   Take the end of a loaf of bread, the piece that has an entire crusty side, and have the student cut off about a quarter of the piece from each side. Peanut butter the pieces to the back of the banana behind the marshmallow head so they look like folded wings. (OPTIONAL: To make the project a little more "gross," the student can put jelly under the bread wings to make it look/feel like bug guts.)

5   Just when the locust is about to be eaten, have the student drizzle honey over the bread. (Don't drizzle the honey until the locust is about to be eaten because it tends to run down over everything.)

6   Enjoy your delicious locust with wild honey.

Memory Work

. . . .

Say the Names of the Twelve Disciples to an Audience

Materials

• Another person (preferably not the instructor) to whom the student can say this memorized list

Directions

Say to the student: "This year, you have learned the names of all twelve of Jesus' disciples. In a moment, we're going to say them for [name of person]. But first, let's review them to keep them in your memory. Remember that first we learned six names, starting with Simon Peter. Let's say those together now."

(Together): Simon Peter, Andrew, James, John, Philip, Thomas.

"Next we learned the other six names; they started with Matthew. Let's say those together now."

(Together): Matthew, James the son of Alphaeus, Thaddeus, Simon, Judas, Bartholomew.

"Great job! Now let's say them all together."

(Together): Simon Peter, Andrew, James, John, Philip, Thomas, Matthew, James the son of Alphaeus, Thaddeus, Simon, Judas, Bartholomew.

Instructor: Now have the student say this list to another person besides you. Give help whenever necessary, and lots of praise and encouragement.

Coloring Page

· ·

John Baptizes People

John lived in the wilderness and had rough hair and clothes. He told the people that God wanted them to turn away from doing bad things, because God's promised king, the Messiah, was coming. To show that they were serious about changing their lives, people let John baptize them in the Jordan River.

Matthew 21:23-27

Lesson 36: Jesus' Crucifixion Is Near

Activities

Game Activity: **Get Rid of** *Chametz*
Science Activity: **Make Your Own Perfume**
Service Activity: **Showing Respect**
Memory Work: **Say the Books of the New Testament to an Audience**
Coloring Page: **A Woman Honors Jesus**

Game Activity

• •

Get Rid of Chametz

Jesus was in Jerusalem for the Passover festival, a week-long celebration that commemorates God's sparing of the Israelites from the last plague on Egypt (see Exodus 12:1–15). Do this activity to show the student one way Jewish families prepare for Passover.

Materials

- Dust cloth for each student
- 10 cubes of bread hidden throughout the room
- Small flashlight for each student
- Snack for afterwards: matzo bread and peanut butter (if you can't find matzo bread, use water biscuits like Carr's Table Water Crackers)

Directions

1 Tell the student, "God told the Israelites to remove any leavened grain, or *chametz* (kha-METS), from their homes before the celebration of the Passover festival. Observant Jews spend the weeks before Passover thoroughly cleaning their homes to remove any bits of yeast or bread made with yeast."
2 Have the student scurry around the house or classroom and dust it thoroughly!
3 Traditionally, after the cleaning of the home, the children search the house to remove any last trace of *chametz* (this search is called *bedikat chametz*) on the evening before Passover. Before the search begins, a blessing is read in Hebrew, called *al biur chametz* (all bee-UR kha-METS) or "on the removal of *chametz*." Read the translation to the student: "Blessed are you Lord, our God, Ruler of the world, who sanctified us through His commandments and commanded us concerning the removal of the *chametz*."

4 Now give the student a flashlight and turn off the lights in the house. (Usually the search is conducted by candlelight, but flashlights are safer.) See if he can find the ten cubes of bread that have been hidden.

5 Once the bread cubes have been found and thrown away, give the snack to the student. The matzo bread is made without yeast. This symbolizes the haste with which the people of Israel left Egypt; there was no time for bread to rise.

Science Activity

Make Your Own Perfume

The woman poured an expensive perfume over Jesus. Make your own perfume—you can even choose the scent. Make one or make them all.

Materials

- 1 bottle rubbing alcohol (handle carefully and keep away from eyes and mouth!)
- 1 baby food jar PER perfume recipe, OR 1 GladWare Mini Round container with lid (4 oz. size) with lid, PER perfume recipe
- Perfume scents (choose one for each perfume you make):
  - 1 orange
  - 10 whole cloves
  - 1 vanilla bean
  - 1 cinnamon stick
  - ½ c. flower petals (heavily scented flowers work best: honeysuckle, rose, lavender, etc.)

Directions

1 Help the student carefully pour rubbing alcohol into a GladWare container until the container is ⅔ full.

2 Have the student choose the perfume scent he would like to create. (If he chooses orange, peel the orange and tear the rind into bits. If he chooses vanilla or cinnamon, you will need to cut the vanilla bean and cinnamon stick in half in order to fit it inside the container.)

3 Add the scented ingredient (orange peel, cinnamon, etc.) to the rubbing alcohol. Put the top on the GladWare container.

4 Let sit for three days. After three days, dab a little bit of the scented alcohol on the student's wrists or on the base of his throat. The alcohol should smell like the scented ingredient because it dissolved some of the scent particles when it was sitting for three days.

5 If you made more than one scent, you might have the student try making his own special scent combination, like vanilla-cinnamon or orange-clove.

Service Activity

Showing Respect

Directions

1 Decide together on two or three things that the student will do all day (or for a specific period of time) to show respect. (These shouldn't just be tiny things, but rather should show over-the-top respect, like the overwhelming care that the woman showed when she poured a whole bottle of expensive perfume over Jesus' head.)
Some suggested actions:
a. Open the door for your parents every time they get near a door.
b. Call your parents sir or ma'am every time you speak to them.
c. Stand up every time your parents come into the room.
d. Bring your parents a pillow any time they sit down.
e. Refill their water glasses every time they take a sip.
f. Every time they carry something, take it away and carry it for them.
g. Draw a portrait of them and put it on the refrigerator.
h. Kneel or bow when your parents speak to you.
Or come up with your own.

2 Now let the student do those chosen actions, for the period of time the two of you chose. Remind him and encourage him if needed.

Memory Work

Say the Books of the New Testament to an Audience

Materials

• Another person (preferably not the instructor) to whom the student can say this memorized list

Directions

Say to the student: "This year, you have learned all of the books of the New Testament. In a moment, we're going to say them for [name of person]. But first, let's review them all to make sure they stay in your memory. The first five New Testament books are Matthew, Mark, Luke, John, and Acts. Let's say those together."

[Together]: *Matthew, Mark, Luke, John, Acts.*

"Then we learned nine more books, the letters that Paul wrote to different groups of people. They were Romans, First and Second Corinthians, Galatians, Ephesians, Philippians, Colossians, First and Second Thessalonians. Let's say those together."

[Together]: *Romans, First and Second Corinthians, Galatians, Ephesians, Philippians, Colossians,*

First and Second Thessalonians.

"Then we learned four more books, the letters Paul sent to specific people. Let's say those together."

[Together]: First and Second Timothy, Titus, Philemon.

"The last set of books was written to different churches and people as messages by God, by different writers. They were Hebrews, James, First and Second Peter, First, Second, and Third John, Jude, Revelation. Let's say those names together."

[Together]: Hebrews, James, First and Second Peter, First, Second, and Third John, Jude, Revelation.

"Now let's say all of them."

Matthew, Mark, Luke, John, Acts, Romans, First and Second Corinthians, Galatians, Ephesians, Philippians, Colossians, First and Second Thessalonians, First and Second Timothy, Titus, Philemon, Hebrews, James, First and Second Peter, First, Second, and Third John, Jude, Revelation.

Instructor: Now have the student say this list to another person besides you. Give help whenever necessary, and lots of praise and encouragement.

Coloring Page
• •
A Woman Honors Jesus

While Jesus was having dinner, this woman poured a bottle of very expensive perfume onto his head. She did this to show how much she cared about Jesus; she gave him the very best she had! His disciples weren't happy that she had done this, but Jesus praised her and said she did it out of love for him.

Matthew 26:1-13

Supplemental Lessons

The Rest of the Story

Supplemental Lesson 1: The King Is on Trial

Activities

History Project: **Make a Roman Governor's Toga**
Game Activity: **Stuffed Animal on Trial**
Optional Drama Activity: **"Pilate Questions Jesus" Play**
Coloring Page: **Pilate Questions Jesus**

History Project

. . . .

Make a Roman Governor's Toga

Materials

- One old white sheet
- 3 yards of wide purple ribbon
- Double-sided tape
- A piece of cord
- An old T-shirt

Directions

1 Tell the student about the toga and the people who wore it. Say, "During the time of Jesus, the Romans ruled over the Jewish people. Pontius Pilate was the Roman who had been put in charge of the land of Judea, where Jerusalem was. When some of the religious leaders wanted to kill Jesus, they needed Pilate's permission to do it, since he was in charge of that region. In this activity you'll make a special piece of clothing called a toga. Pilate would have worn something like this. After you've made it, you can wear it as a costume for the Trial activity later this week."

"A toga was a complicated outfit to wear and was usually only worn on important occasions. Traditionally the toga was two and a half times as long as the person was tall and about two times as wide as the person. Slaves were forbidden from ever wearing a toga, because the toga was considered to be a sign of power and prestige. Our toga will have a purple edge. Purple was an expensive color to make in ancient times, so having a lot of purple on your clothes was a mark of being a rich or important person."

2   Help the student fold the sheet in half lengthwise. Have her use the double-sided tape to attach the purple ribbon along one side of the long edge. You can sew it yourself instead if you feel it would work better. Help the student trim away any excess ribbon.

3   Have the student put on the T-shirt and use the piece of cord to tie a belt around her waist.

4   Stand behind the student, holding the toga by the long straight edge. Drape a quarter of the toga over the student's left shoulder and arm, then have her move the toga up her arm, so that her hand is free.

5   Help the child bring the rest of the toga around her body, making sure that she brings it under her right arm. Have her gather a couple of folds in the toga and tuck them into the waistband securely.

6   Last of all, help the child fold the remaining loose fabric over her left arm. Tell the child she will need to keep her left arm close to her body to hold it in position.

Game Activity

Stuffed Animal on Trial

Like a modern judge, Pilate was trying to figure out the guilt or innocence of the person who was accused of a crime. This game helps the child understand the concept of a trial. (Remember that the stuffed animal, not the student, is the "criminal.")

Materials

- Stuffed animal
- Index cards
- Pencil

1   Tell the student to go get a stuffed animal. This will be the prisoner on trial.

2   Give the student a number of index cards. On each card you have written something the animal may have "stolen." The student will pick one or two, but won't show you which ones have been selected. The theft of this item will be the stuffed animal's "crime." *(Possible items: apple, toothbrush, lightbulb, wallet, book, box of animal crackers, purse, cookie, magic marker, T-shirt, ball, kite, scissors, sandwich, Hot Wheels car)*

3   You act as the judge and ask questions to find out what's on the card. (As in the game "20 Questions," you must ask one thing at a time: "Is this thing round?" "Would this thing be good to eat?")

4   With a group, each student can ask the "criminal" one question, and the group could decide together what's on the card—that would be more like a jury trial.

· ·
"Pilate Questions Jesus" Play

Reenact the scene of Jesus' interrogation by Pilate with a class. You can act this out with as few as three actors.

Materials

- "Pilate Questions Jesus" script (Student Page 389)
- Costumes: Pilate can wear the Roman governor's toga from the previous activity. The soldiers can wear the centurion's helmet from Lesson 10.

Cast of characters (starred ones are necessary):
JESUS *
PILATE *
CROWD * (1 or more people)
BARABBAS
2 SOLDIERS that escort Jesus

Directions

1 Tear out Student Page 389, and give a copy of it to each actor who will have a speaking role.
2 Read through the script at least one time for the actors to get used to their lines (you should highlight their parts for them).
3 Practice the scene at least one time, showing the actors where to stand.
4 Perform the play (for yourselves or in front of an audience).

Coloring Page
· ·
Pilate Questions Jesus

The Roman governor, Pilate, asked Jesus questions to see if Jesus was a rebel leader. Jesus said he was a different kind of king. He came to show people the truth about God, not to fight a war against the Romans.

Script: Pilate Questions Jesus

(The SOLDIERS bring JESUS and BARABBAS to PILATE. They continue to guard BARABBAS while JESUS and PILATE talk to each other.)

PILATE: Are you the king of the Jews?

JESUS: Is that your own idea, or did others talk to you about me?

PILATE (annoyed): It was YOUR people and your chief priests who handed you over to me. What is it you have done?

JESUS: My kingdom is not of this world. If it were, my servants would fight to prevent my arrest by the Jews. But now my kingdom is from another place.

PILATE: You are a king, then!

JESUS: You are right in saying I am a king. In fact, for this reason I was born, and for this I came into the world, to testify to the truth. Everyone on the side of truth listens to me.

PILATE: What is truth?

PILATE (says to crowd): I find no basis for a charge against him. But it is your custom for me to release to you one prisoner at the time of the Passover. Do you want me to release "the king of the Jews"?

CROWD: No, not him! Give us Barabbas!

PILATE: What shall I do with Jesus who is called the Christ?

CROWD: Crucify him! Crucify him!

PILATE: Why? What crime has he committed?

CROWD: Crucify him!

PILATE: I am innocent of this man's blood. It is your responsibility!

(JESUS is led away to be crucified. The soldiers let BARABBAS go free; he is excited to be freed.)

John 18:33–40

John 18:33-40

Supplemental Lesson 2: The Crucifixion

Activities

History Project: **Make Pilate's Sign**
Science Activity: **Plant a Seed**
Cooking Project: **Hot Cross Buns**
Coloring Page: **Jesus Is Crucified**

History Project
. . . .
Make Pilate's Sign

Pilate wrote "Jesus of Nazareth, King of the Jews" in Aramaic, Latin, and Greek and placed the sign on the cross of Jesus. Make a similar sign and learn a little bit of another language.

Materials

- Pilate's sign in Aramaic, Latin, and Greek (Student Page 397)
- Glue stick
- Scissors
- Cardboard or cardstock, 9" x 12"

Directions

1 Tell the student that Pontius Pilate had a sign made to hang on Jesus' cross. It said, "Jesus of Nazareth, King of the Jews." The phrase was written in three languages, so everyone who walked by Jesus would know what the sign read.

2 Turn to Student Page 397. Show the student that the first line says "Jesus of Nazareth, King of the Jews" in Latin. Teach the student how to pronounce it: "YAY soos naza RAY noos rex joo day OH room."

3 Show the student that the second line says "Jesus of Nazareth, King of the Jews" in Greek. Teach the student how to pronounce it. "YEH soos hoh nah zoh RAI ohs hoh bah zil EH oos tohn eeYOU dai ohn."

4 Show the student that the third line says "Jesus of Nazareth, King of the Jews" in Aramaic (a language related to Hebrew; most Jews spoke Aramaic during Jesus' time). Teach the student how to pronounce it: "yeh SHOO ah ha nots RAI uh MEH lek hah yeh hoo DEEM."

5   Now tear out the Student Page, and have the student cut out the three lines of script.
6   Glue the script to the cardboard to make the sign that was on Jesus' cross. *Note to Instructor: This sign goes by different names. Sometimes it is called by the Latin term for "inscription or label," titulus. Sometimes, especially in artwork where it wouldn't be practical to write out the whole sign, it is abbreviated INRI (from Iesus Nazarenus, Rex Iudaeorum).*

Science Activity

• •

Plant a Seed

Materials

- Dry beans
- A bowl
- Several small cups or jars
- Potting soil
- Water

Directions

Say to the student: "Jesus died and was buried, but that wasn't the end of his story! He had told his followers, long before his death, that he would die and come back to life (Matthew 20:17–19, Mark 8:31). In John 12:23–24, he compared himself to a seed or a kernel of grain that must be put into the ground (and even 'die') in order to bring something new, that wasn't there before. This week we're going to plant a seed, and bury it in the dirt, and watch for it to come back up as a new plant! When you see a new plant spring up where there was only dirt before, think of Jesus coming back from being dead."

1   Soak nine or ten dry beans overnight in a bowl, with enough water to cover all the beans.
2   Have the student half-fill several small cups or jars with soil.
3   Have the student use his fingers to dig a 1½-inch deep hole in each cup.
4   Place one bean in each hole and cover it lightly with soil.
5   Water the soil and leave the cups where they can get plenty of sunlight.
6   Check the cups each day, and keep the soil moist. Some of the beans should sprout in just a few days.

Note to Instructor: If you follow these directions, at least some of the seeds should sprout. If none do, be sure to remind the child that unlike these failed seeds, Jesus actually did rise again. These plants are a helpful reminder but not the real thing.

Cooking Project

. . . .

Hot Cross Buns

Hot cross buns are sweet spiced buns with an icing "cross" on top. No one knows for sure who invented these buns, but they have become a traditional Good Friday and Easter treat in Britain and many other countries. The cross atop each bun is supposed to remind the eater of Jesus' cross. Have the child assist you in as many steps of the recipe as possible.

Ingredients

- ¾ c. warm water (110 degrees F.)
- 3 Tbsp. butter
- 1 Tbsp. powdered milk
- ¼ c. sugar
- ⅜ tsp. salt
- 1 egg
- 1 egg white
- 3 c. all-purpose flour
- 1 Tbsp. active dry yeast
- ¾ c. dried raisins (or try other bits of dried fruit)
- 1 tsp. ground cinnamon
- 1 egg yolk
- 2 Tbsp. water

For the crosses:
- 2 tsp. milk
- ½ c. powdered sugar
- ¼ tsp. vanilla extract

Directions

1 Have the student help you mix together warm water, butter, powdered milk, sugar, salt, egg, egg white, flour, and yeast, and then begin kneading. For the last 5 minutes of kneading, add cinnamon and the raisins/dried fruit.

2 Set aside in a covered, oiled bowl until doubled in size. Punch down on floured surface, cover, and let rest 10 minutes.

3 Shape into 12 balls and place in a greased 9" x 12" pan. Cover and let rise in a warm place till double, about 35–40 minutes.

4 Preheat oven to 375 degrees F. Mix egg yolk and 2 tablespoons water. Brush on dough balls.

5 Bake for 20 minutes. Remove from pan immediately and cool on wire rack.

6 To make crosses: Mix together powdered sugar, vanilla, and milk. Have the student dip a brush into this mixture and brush an "X" onto each cooled bun.

Coloring Page
· ·
Jesus Is Crucified

The Roman governor and some of the Jewish religious leaders had Jesus killed. They hung him on a cross to die next to criminals. The soldiers kept his clothes, and his friends were very sad. But his death wasn't the end. It was part of God's plan to take away people's sins.

Pilate's Sign

Pilate, the Roman governor, had a sign hung on Jesus' cross when Jesus was crucified. It said "Jesus of Nazareth, King of the Jews" in three languages (Latin, Greek, and Aramaic), so that everyone could read it. Latin was the language used by the Romans, Aramaic was spoken by Jesus and most of the Jewish people, and many people from different countries could speak Greek.

Latin

IESVS NAZARENVS REX IVDÆORVM

Greek

Ἰησοῦς ὁ Ναζωραῖος ὁ βασιλεὺς τῶν Ἰουδαίων

Aramaic

ישוע הנצרי ומלך היהודים

John 19:17–27

Supplemental Lesson 3: Jesus Is Alive Again

Activities

Game Activity: **Stone Hunt**
Art History Project: **Tanner's** *Two Disciples at the Tomb*
Coloring Page: **Jesus Is Alive!**

Game Activity

• •

Stone Hunt

This is a fun seek-and-find game that reinforces the concept that the stone was rolled away and Jesus is alive. There is a small amount of advance preparation needed, but it takes only a minute.

Materials

- 8 palm-sized smooth stones (Can't find these? Oven-bake some salt-dough in stone shapes. See Lesson 7 for a salt-dough recipe)
- Medium-tip black Sharpie marker
- Bowl or basket to hold the stones

Directions

1   Before class time, use the Sharpie to write one word on each stone: *The, tomb, is, empty, because, Jesus, is, alive!* (Make sure you capitalize *The* and put an exclamation point after *alive.*)
2   Put the stones in a basket. When class begins, tell the student you have a message scrambled up. See if she can rearrange the stones to read the correct message: *The tomb is empty because Jesus is alive!* Prompt her by telling her that a sentence begins with a capital letter and ends with a mark of punctuation.
3   Now have the student put her head down while you hide the stones.
4   Once the stones are hidden, see if the student can find all the stones and put them back in the right order.

Art History Project

. . . .

Tanner's *Two Disciples at the Tomb*

Most depictions of the empty tomb show the angel appearing to the women in Luke 24, but Tanner's painting Two Disciples at the Tomb *captures the moment from this week's lesson: the reactions of John and Peter when they first see the tomb is empty.*

Materials

- Tanner's *Two Disciples at the Tomb* (Student Page 403)

Directions

Show the student the painting on Student Page 403 as you say the following. Encourage the student to answer the questions in complete sentences.

1   This painting is by Henry Ossawa Tanner, who also painted the picture of the angel appearing to Mary that we saw back in Lesson 21.
2   How many people are in this painting? (There are two people.)
3   This is a painting of the story from the lesson. These men are both disciples. We heard the name of one of the disciples in the Bible verses from this week. Do you remember that name? (He is Peter OR Simon Peter.) [The student may not remember this detail. In that case, read John 20:2–3 aloud.]
4   John, the other disciple, was younger than Peter. Remember how he outran Peter and got to the tomb first? Which man in the painting is John? (The one in front without the beard is John.)
5   Peter stands behind him. Where is Peter's hand resting? (It is on his chest OR on his heart.)
6   Do you see the entrance to the tomb? Point to the entrance. Can you see the stone that has been rolled away from the entrance?
7   The disciples' faces are lit up. Where is the light coming from? (It is coming from inside the tomb.)
8   Where is John looking? (He is looking into the tomb.)
9   Do you remember from the story which disciple believed right away that Jesus must be alive? (John believed.) That is why he is the one looking straight into the tomb, his face shining with the light. Peter looks down at the ground, as if he did not understand right away.

Coloring Page

. . . .

Jesus Is Alive!

Jesus was dead, but when his disciples came to his grave on the third day after he died, they found that he was alive again! Peter and another disciple looked in and found that Jesus wasn't in his grave anymore.

Two Disciples at the Tomb by Henry Ossawa Tanner

Used by permission of the Art Institute of Chicago

John 20:1–9